ELVIS COSTELLO

Other titles in the series:

Beck
The Clash
Leonard Cohen
Tom Waits
Neil Young

ELVIS COSTELLO

David Sheppard

THUNDER'S
MOUTH
PRESS

Published in the United States by
Thunder's Mouth Press
841 Broadway, Fourth Floor
New York, NY 10003

First published in Great Britain by Unanimous Ltd
12 The Ivories, 6–8 Northampton Street, London N1 2HY

Text editor: Ian Fitzgerald
Project editor: Nicola Birtwisle

Library of Congress Card Number: 00-108284

ISBN: 1-56025-303-7

Printed in Italy

1 2 3 4 5 6 7 8 9

Acknowledgements

I'd like to extend my gratitude to Simon Majumdar and Nicola Birtwisle for
damming my torrents with such finesse. David Belcher and Keiron Phelan helped me
in ways too abstract to recount here. Thanks too to Vinita Joshi for her patience and
to Louise Clarke for her emotional toothpaste etc... Costello-ites who haven't yet
done so should bury themselves in Brian Hinton's excellent *Let Them All Talk*. His
aim is true.

CONTENTS

ONE

THE STORY

Adopting the King of rock 'n' roll's name was always the most impudent of acts – to do it in the year that the musical monarch's reign finally came to its tragic conclusion only served to compound the felony. And although Declan Patrick MacManus would later seek to bury the name under a variety of aliases – Little Hands Of Concrete, Napoleon Dynamite, The Emotional Toothpaste, The Imposter, Coward Brother – for his army of fans, Elvis Costello is a kind of king too, although of a very different sort.

A shrewd sense of timing and the almost alchemical ability to fashion career-enhancing gold from the base metal of unlikely circumstance are Elvis Costello fortes. How else could a myopic singer-songwriter with a job as a computer operator, a wife and child and a penchant for the rustic lamentations of The Band somehow become a punk rock hero, only to end up penning songs with Paul McCartney and Burt Bacharach?

Some critics claim that he is a musical mercenary, willing to embrace any genre if there is a chance of success in it. But this is to miss the point – Elvis Costello is a man with a prodigious musical talent that must express itself in any way it can.

Costello's story begins on 25 August 1954, when he was born

in St Mary's Hospital, Paddington, London, to big band crooner Ronald 'Ross' MacManus and his wife Lillian Costello.

Ross and Lillian had recently relocated to Twickenham, West London, from their native Birkenhead, just a ten-minute ferry ride across the River Mersey from then-thriving Liverpool. Both parents belonged to Merseyside's Irish community, although both had been born in the Liverpool area.

Theirs was a Catholic, socialist but above all musical family. Ross' father had been a ship's musician on some of the great ocean liners that sailed the Atlantic between the wars, and was one of the first people to introduce early American blues records to the UK. Ross MacManus had inherited his father's musical gene and was talented enough to support the family with a professional singing career.

By the time of Declan's birth Ross was a regular performer with the hugely popular Joe Loss Orchestra, Britain's answer to the Glenn Miller big band. A major part of the orchestra's remit was to play the hits of the day. As a result, frontman Ross MacManus spent much of his free time learning the latest transatlantic smashes or the hits of Frank Sinatra and Tony Bennett. Simultaneously, Lillian MacManus found work running the record department at the prestigious department store Selfridges on Oxford Street, where her tastes ran to jazz of various hues.

Unsurprisingly, then, the MacManus household was awash with music.

Life proceeded agreeably enough for the family throughout the 1950s and early 1960s, with Declan attending a local junior school. But even from an early age Declan's musical development outstripped that of his peers. The precocious nine-year-old jazz buff was always racing home from the playground to indulge an early predilection for the records of Mel Torme and Ella Fitzgerald, an implausibly mature taste for one so young. As a result, he remained something of a loner throughout his school years.

Although the early 1960s beat boom ultimately meant decline for lumbering ensembles like The Joe Loss Orchestra, it was also the age of their last hurrah. Especially as the big bands were adept at reinterpreting the brash new pop sounds in their own easy-listening style. *The Joe Loss Show*, on BBC Radio's *Light Programme*, actually became a showcase for many of the emerging bands of the 1960s. A great treat for the pre-adolescent Declan MacManus was to sit in on these Friday afternoon performances and rub shoulders with the likes of The Hollies, The Merseybeats, Engelbert Humperdinck and even The Beatles, the latter of whom were steadily monopolizing his attentions.

School held little interest for Declan. His main focus was his phonograph or the guitar his father had bought him from a Richmond electrical shop for his twelfth birthday. Having mastered some basic chords, Declan rapidly began penning his own rudimentary songs. It was, after all, 1966 – the year of Dylan's *Blonde On Blonde*, The Beatles' *Revolver* and The Beach Boys' *Pet Sounds*.

In the years that followed, Declan and his father's shared regard for the hit parade began to diverge – though not in the expected manner. Rather than the son suddenly becoming smitten with the rapidly unfolding psychedelic revolution while the father reverted to more conservative musical idioms, the opposite was the case. The still relatively young Ross MacManus actually dabbled in hippydom, growing his hair and attempting (and initially failing) to turn his son on to the mind-altering delights of chemically inclined West Coast bands such as The Jefferson Airplane and The Grateful Dead.

At the same time, Ross MacManus' best known performance (at least as far as British audiences are concerned) was recorded. The jingle that accompanied a memorable advert for R White's Lemonade may not be the finest piece of British pop music to emerge from the early 1970s but, as sung by MacManus Snr, it is certainly one of the most lovingly remembered.

While his father tuned in (and to some extent dropped out), Declan turned his back on acid rock and began a studious analysis of soul – Motown, especially Marvin Gaye, along with Stax/Atlantic stars Otis Redding and Aretha Franklin, were his new fixations. Bob Dylan and his acolytes The Band also began to interest the inquisitive teenager and helped lead him through a complex genealogy of influences back to the blues of Robert Johnson and Skip James and latterly to obscure American singer-songwriters like David Accles, David Blue and Jesse Winchester.

Partly as a result of his unlikely dalliances with the counter-culture, Ross MacManus' marriage to Lillian foundered and the couple separated at the close of the 1960s, with Lillian and the sixteen-year-old Declan decamping to Birkenhead, while Ross stayed on in London to attend to what was now a solo career.

Before his move back to Merseyside Declan made his first public appearance as a singer. This took place at the Crypt of St Elizabeth's church, Richmond. The little subterranean chamber was home to the local folk club. The night of Declan's tenderfoot appearance happened to coincide with a visit from British folk eminence Ewan McColl (writer of the standard 'The First Time Ever I Saw Your Face' and father of pop star Kirsty McColl). However, Declan's was not an auspicious debut. On the contrary, McColl spent the duration of the youngster's set with his head lolling on his chest, dozing.

In the meantime, Declan's musical attention turned to country music, or more accurately to the country-rock hybrid pioneered by the Byrds and Gram Parsons. He also immersed himself in the purer, rootsier sounds of George Jones, Merle Haggard and Hank Williams. His other love of the era was The Band, the Canadian quintet who had previously been Bob Dylan's backing group and who, by the late 1960s, had emerged as a ground-breaking act in their own right.

Liverpool at the turn of the 1970s was not the thriving musical hotspot it had once been. In fact, Declan found himself drawn away from the city's becalmed musical scene towards a new obsession – football. After moving back to Merseyside Declan began a life-long love for Liverpool Football Club.

However, the future star had not completely abandoned his musical aspirations. To further his ambitions he hooked up with a friend, Allan Mayes, three years his senior, whom he had first met during a 1969 Liverpool holiday. The occasion of this latter encounter was a dreary New Year's Eve party in 1971 during which the two teenagers found themselves engrossed in discussion about the relative merits of various pop groups.

The eighteen-year-old Mayes was already something of a veteran on Liverpool's progressive rock scene. Music predicated on lyrical whimsy, twenty-minute songs and eternal guitar solos hardly seemed the most attractive proposition for the serially rootsy and rather purist Declan, but the unlikely pair soon hit it off. By the end of the night they were ensconced in a bedroom, hunched over guitars, duetting their way through every song they could remember.

Mayes was in a band, Rusty, who were in need of a second guitarist. Declan got the job – and before long had promoted himself to joint singer-guitarist. Under his influence the group's emphasis quickly moved away from rock and began to gravitate towards the folk-soul idiom then practised by the likes of Van Morrison and The Band. By the time of their first gig together at Liverpool's Lamplight Folk club at the end of January 1972 not only had Rusty added spirited versions of songs by Morrison, Neil Young and Bob Dylan to their Allan Mayes originals, they were also playing a brand new Band-style Declan MacManus song entitled 'Warm House'.

By this time, Declan had found a job. As if predicting a 1977 music press description of the angry young Elvis Costello's image as being that of a 'psychotic bank clerk', the position actually was with a banking organization – a central clearing house for savings and mortgage outlets. Though given the then-glamorous title of 'IBM 360 Computer Operator', his main duty was simply to feed tapes into a living room-sized main-frame processor. The only bonus was that the work was slow – giving Declan plenty of time to work on his songs. One draw-back was that the constant exposure to flickering screens and brutal strip-lighting gave him persistent headaches and a doc-tor eventually diagnosed astigmatism – a minor affliction, but one that would only be relieved by prescription spectacles. An image was beginning to form.

By the spring of 1972 Rusty had thrown off the last vestiges of progressive rock. They'd also thrown off all their other members, leaving Allan Mayes and Declan MacManus to their American-derived singer-songwriting. They had begun to get regular bookings as a duo and, free from the strictures of a noisy rock band, Mayes and MacManus' vocal harmonizing began to take centre stage.

The pair were also becoming influenced by London-based Band soundalikes Brinsley Schwarz. When the group played Liverpool's Cavern Club in early 1972 Declan managed to sit in on their soundcheck and cornered their bass player, Nick Lowe, for a nervy chat. The band's witty self-deprecation and informal style had a profound effect on the impressionable sev-enteen-year-old.

As 1972 unfolded Rusty began broadening their horizons. Not only were they bulking out their live sets with Brinsley Schwarz songs but they were playing on the group's home turf of London, too. In the summer of 1972 they got a big break when they were asked to open the bill at a London concert headlined by English folk star Ralph McTell.

Even the briefest re-exposure to the London music scene was

enough to turn Declan's head. The duo briefly changed their name to Procyon, for no good reason, but even this wasn't enough to keep the ever-more-ambitious Declan in Liverpool. After honouring a clutch of contracted dates – including a swansong supporting Cockney Rebel at Warwick University – he and Allan Mayes went their separate ways, the latter back to Liverpool and anonymity, the former to London, the orbit of Brinsley Schwarz and thence the world.

With his father's Twickenham home and a serious girlfriend, Mary Burgoyne (whom he had met in Liverpool the previous year) waiting, Declan moved south permanently in the spring of 1973.

To pay his way he once again found employ as a computer operator – this time at the West London payroll centre of the cosmetic firm Elizabeth Arden. In April 1973 he made his first solo performance at a Thames-side Twickenham pub called the Barmy Arms. The main point of interest in this gig is that Declan was now performing as DP Costello. The name change was both a nod to his mother's side of the family and to his American musical heroes: his favourite Gram Parsons album was called *GP*.

Once settled in the capital, Costello homed in on Brinsley Schwarz with the tenacity of a groupie and the devotion of a trainspotter. Throughout the summer of 1973 he was to be found at every one of the band's regular London gigs, hanging out at soundchecks, between sets and after shows. Within months he had become a kind of factotum-cum-junior roadie and, more significantly, had begun to forge a genuine bond with the band's most charismatic member, Nick Lowe.

At a summer 1973 Brinsley Schwarz show at St Pancras Town Hall, Costello met bassist Michael Kent and instantly found a like-minded, American-literate, Brinsley Schwarz-influenced musician. Kent knew a drummer, Malcolm Dennis, and within days the trio were rehearsing under the name

Mothertruckers and had booked a couple of trial gigs at South London colleges. After a spell as The Bizario Brothers they finally settled on the terse Flip City.

Flip City soon evolved into a five-piece, then did the fashionable thing for an early '70s band and moved in together. They couldn't afford to do as their heroes The Band (and briefly Brinsley Schwarz) had done and relocate to a rural idyll in order to, as the argot of the time had it, get their shit together. Instead they rented a Victorian house in the sleepy West London suburb of Roehampton for the princely sum of £8 a week.

The environment proved conducive to Costello's songwriting – his ideas quickly evolving from bedroom to stage – and Flip City were soon enmeshed in the thriving London semi-pro circuit. From the middle of 1974 the climate for the band should have improved further still with the unpredicted rise of what was later dubbed pub rock. A grass roots reaction to the grandiose bathos of stadium rock acts like Pink Floyd and Led Zeppelin, the pub rock scene was both the precursor to and the catalyst for the punk explosion that followed. With its musical roots in driving American R&B and its adopted attitude that of casual irreverence, pub rock was relatively easy to execute (no tortuous guitar solos to learn, no gargantuan lighting rigs to install) and found a willing metropolitan audience keen to sup to good-time music that at least retained some vestige of roots integrity.

That Flip City didn't fully capitalize on the pub rock scene is partly down to the band's modest abilities – they were always more enthusiastic than gifted – and more significantly to Costello's own growing disillusionment with their frailties. Not for the first, or last time, the practical advantages of coexisting with fellow-traveller musicians were beginning to be outweighed by the band's inability to keep pace with Costello's spiralling ambition.

In the meantime, his mind was briefly on other matters. Mary Burgoyne was pregnant, and in November 1974 she and Costello were married, with the couple moving into a flat immediately below Costello's father and his new wife Sarah in Twickenham. A son, Matthew, was born in January 1975 and the new family upped sticks again, this time to an address in Whitton, Middlesex.

At this time, Costello embarked on his first recording session – a demo tape by Flip City made at Dave Robinson's rudimentary Hope and Anchor studios in Islington, North London. The six songs contained a clutch of sluggishly polite cover versions and Costello originals like 'Pay It Back' (unrecognizable from its later *My Aim Is True* incarnation) and 'I'm Packing Up'. The sound was feeble and the playing reticent. Only the singer was anything like convincing: Costello's noticeably Americanized, Graham Parker-esque burr was prevalent throughout – and on the set's best number, 'Imagination Is A Powerful Deceiver', the feral potency of his later work was already manifest.

Flip City dissolved in November 1975. But by the beginning of the following year Costello had wangled himself a weekly Friday night residency at Putney's Half Moon Club, beginning (inauspiciously) on 13 February and lasting to the end of March. Costello's role was essentially that of a glorified master of ceremonies, though the evening demanded he play several short sets – the perfect environment in which to blood new songs. His fee (fifty pence a night, plus all the stale sandwiches he could eat) may have been paltry, but in all other regards this was the beginning of a hugely fruitful period for DP Costello, as he was again billing himself.

One major benefit of regularly playing solo to a noisy, boozy crowd was the effect it had on his stagecraft. Already the possessor of a megaphone voice and ready between-song wit, Costello was now dispensing with folksy strumming in favour of the driving, bludgeoning guitar style with which he would machete his way through the first four years of his public career.

In the spring of 1976, the Putney residency ended and Costello turned his attention to landing a recording contract. Borrowing a Revox reel-to-reel tape recorder from a friend, he put together a demo tape of some of his songs – two of which would find their way onto his debut album. Raw, unadorned and razor-sharp, the tape is by turns impassioned and poignant. Costello, seizing the moment, sent a copy of his demo to Radio London DJ and pub rock champion Charlie Gillett. Costello had spent the year badgering Gillett to make on-air announcements of his upcoming gigs, and now he persuaded him to broadcast his home-made recordings. The wilderness years were nearing their end.

Impressed, Gillett offered to release a DP Costello record on his own independent label, Oval. Flattered by the offer but already guessing that bigger fish were circling, Costello politely declined. Within weeks of the broadcast, Virgin Records came in with a bid – and Costello rejected that one, too. Eventually, he decided to sign to the newly-formed Stiff Records. The label was the brainchild of former Brinsley Schwarz and Kilburn And The High Roads manager Dave Robinson and his partner Andrew Jakeman – or, as he called himself, Jake Riviera. Robinson and Riviera set up Stiff initially as a vehicle for their friend, the now-solo Nick Lowe. However, with the signing of Costello it looked as if they were set for bigger things.

Robinson and Riviera had been alerted to Costello's talents not via Charlie Gillett's radio show but by more direct means. In August 1976 they had released the label's debut single, Nick Lowe's 'And So It Goes', and Costello had journeyed to Stiff's headquarters in order to procure a copy. He made the venture worth his while by bringing along a four-track selection from his home-recorded demo, which he duly left on Jake Riviera's desk. Dave Robinson was vaguely aware of Costello's work from Flip City days, but to Riviera the name on the tape box meant nothing.

It was the first demo that Stiff had received directly and Riviera spooled it onto the reel-to-reel expecting the worst. To his delight the songs couldn't have been further from the usual demo fodder. His first instinct was to try and sign the writer of these sophisticated songs to supply material for the burgeoning Stiff roster. On further listening, however, he and Robinson quickly realized that Costello's delivery was equally compelling. Costello was ushered into the Stiff offices and signed with the label soon after. Riviera, showing his true ex-advertising colours, quickly set about a scheme that would successfully launch Stiff's twenty-one-year-old charge upon an unsuspecting public.

Riviera saw the christian name 'Elvis' as a sardonic and appropriate soubriquet for an artist steeped in American rock 'n' roll, with aspirations for the genre's pinnacle. Tacit in Costello's appropriation of the name was the audacious idea that the young pretender was somehow out to steal the monarch's slipping crown. To add to the implicit geekiness of the name, Riviera encouraged Costello to accentuate his myopic and somewhat scrawny appearance. To this end he had the singer fitted with outsized spectacle frames and squeezed him into one-size-too-small thrift-store suits. He also urged him to play up the angrier and more vitriolic elements that shot through his recent songwriting. As a result, early publicity pictures show Costello looking like a scowling seven-stone weakling. Riviera's plan worked – a 1976 press release describes Costello as looking like 'Buddy Holly on acid' and it's this image, for all his subsequent visual makeovers, that most still associate with the name Elvis Costello.

As for Costello's debut LP, Riviera and Robinson drafted in

American band Clover, whom the duo were currently managing. A laid back country-rock outfit, they would later find fame as Huey Lewis And The News. Costello spent a weekend with Clover at their Headley Grange base, teaching them his songs before the ensemble regrouped at Pathway Studios with Nick Lowe at the helm.

The album took a total of twenty-four hours' studio time, spread over a couple of weeks in October and cost approximately £2,000. The sessions had to be segmented as Costello was still working full-time at Elizabeth Arden and could only make a couple of the recording dates by phoning in and feigning sickness. Even during such a brief studio sojourn the ensemble managed to cut a quartet of other Costello originals, as well as the thirteen-track entirety of *My Aim Is True*.

The first fruits of the Clover sessions appeared as Costello's debut single, 'Less Than Zero' – Stiff's eleventh release – which hit the shops on 25 March 1977. It had taken the tenacious Declan Patrick MacManus seven years of unquenchable self-belief but finally his name, or at least a version of it, was finally on the sleeve of a real vinyl record – albeit one that failed to chart.

More significant was the curious compilation album, *A Bunch Of Stiffs*, released a week later, in which (a remixed) 'Less Than Zero' vied for attention with tracks by hippy-relic Magic Michael, an uncredited Graham Parker and Welsh pop classicist Dave Edmunds. Amid this plethora of wry whimsicality and unreconstructed R&B, Costello's fulminating rant about notorious British fascist Sir Oswald Mosley stood out like a sore thumb and immediately marked him as – The Damned aside – Stiff's punk-crossover-most-likely.

At the end of May he played his first solo show as Elvis Costello, supporting The (Graham Parker-less) Rumour (there must have been a frisson at finally sharing a stage with ex-members of Brinsley Schwarz) at London's Nashville Rooms. It was a markedly changed performer from the Flip City or even DP Costello versions that preceded it. Tearing through a dozen songs from the forthcoming album accompanied by just his own scything Fender Jazzmaster electric guitar, this was a souped up twenty-one-year-old firebrand, part 1966-era Dylan, part adrenalin punk rocker, part amphetamine soul belter.

Given the climate and Costello's raging onstage predisposition, 'Alison' was perhaps an odd choice for a second single. A slow, soulful ballad about love and betrayal with a heartbreaking chorus, the song remains an early Costello classic. Its closing mantra also provided him with the title for his debut LP. The more far-sighted of contemporary commentators wondered if all punk records might one day sound this way. Nevertheless, once again the single failed to chart.

With a couple of singles and an album under his belt, Costello's next move was to put together a band to take his songs on the road. First on board was drummer Pete Thomas. Formerly of Chilli Willi And The Red Hot Peppers, Thomas was introduced to Costello by Jake Riviera. Next up was bassist Bruce Thomas, an erstwhile Steely Dan fan who failed his first audition for Costello – his combination of long hair and jazz-rock leanings proving too unpalatable to the new wave trailblazer. Thomas went away, cut his hair and learned Costello's two singles by heart. He then auditioned again and got the job.

Keyboardist Steve Nason completed the line-up. Classically trained at the Royal College of Music, Nason was swiftly re-christened Steve Naive (later the more punk-looking 'Nieve') due to his scant knowledge of rock 'n' roll history. However, his musicianship was to prove to be invaluable to this odd-looking group, which styled itself, ironically, The Attractions.

The combo made its live debut on 14 July at the Woods Leisure Centre in Plymouth. It was essentially just a live try-out, but the swelling interest in the intriguing Costello phenomenon meant a clutch of music press reporters had been dispatched to cover the event. The general impression was a good one. In their shiny suits and skinny ties the band may have looked like a pilled-up version of the Merseybeats, but the sound they made was something else entirely.

Inspired by the positive reaction of the music press, Costello left his job at Elizabeth Arden to become a full-time musician.

As a last throw of the singles dice before the album was unleashed, another song from the Clover session, '(The Angels Wanna Wear My) Red Shoes', was released at the end of July and Riviera booked a UK tour to promote it. He also arranged for Costello and The Attractions to play on a flat-bed truck outside the Hilton Hotel in Park Lane, where executives from CBS were gathering for their annual international conference. The stunt was designed to get Costello noticed, and it worked: by the end of 1977 he had been signed by Columbia in the US.

In the meantime *My Aim Is True* was released. Packaged with lurid op-art visuals by one Barney Bubbles, the LP at least looked the very epitome of 1977 new wave chic. On the front cover Costello appears mean and lean with spiked hair, drainpipe jeans and angry sneer. The psycho-nerd image still had a lot of mileage left in it and the cover art only helped to emphasize the splenetic nature of the songs inside. Yet the cover, like the album itself, also hinted at rock 'n' roll classicism, and amongst a plethora of releases by plagiaristic punk arrivistes, Costello's LP came with an aura of ineffable significance.

With its themes of mangled love affairs, sexual and general impotence and spiteful revenge, *My Aim Is True* is an album of its time that also belongs in the canon of great rock 'n' roll debuts. Arguably better than Dylan or Springsteen's freshman LPs, Costello's debut had the critics reaching for the lexicons. The *NME* described it as 'something of metallic beauty', while the *Melody Maker* saw another side: 'you can dance to it, swoon and romance with it, smooch and romance to it'. They never said that about *Never Mind The Bollocks: Here's The Sex Pistols*.

Suddenly everything seemed to be going Costello's way. A summer tour of the UK and a session for DJ John Peel's influential BBC Radio 1 show helped. As did an interview in the *NME* with revered rock writer Nick Kent, which was something akin to a seal of musical approval from one of rock's most respected taste-makers.

Kent provided the perfect conduit through which Costello could publicly banish the past and recast himself as an angry twenty-two-year-old iconoclast with a burning mission. In the interview Costello came across as both ambitious and vindictive. He admitted to going through the guest lists at gigs and scrubbing out the names of anyone who had rebuffed him in the past. He claimed to be motivated by 'revenge and guilt' and made reference to a, possibly apocryphal, 'little black book' full of the names of those against whom he soon hoped to exact vengeance. For added effect, he pulled a large rusty nail from his pocket, explaining that it was his chosen weapon of defence. Kent took it all in – concurring when Costello described himself unironically as 'a genius' – and generally failing to call the young upstart on any of his manifest posturing. It all helped cement the singer's essential street cred.

However, it was not all a publicity stunt, as anyone who caught Costello and The Attractions' gigs that summer must have realized. Venomous and enraged, he really did seem to be drawing on great reserves of hate every time he spat out his songs. The more unreceptive the audience, the more fulminating – and at times genuinely threatening – was his presence.

Buoyed by the critical success of *My Aim Is True,* Robinson and Riviera put together a 'Stiff's Greatest Stiffs Live' tour, with Costello performing alongside fellow new wave rising stars Ian

Dury And The Blockheads, as well as old pub rockers such as Wreckless Eric and Nick Lowe.

As the tour progressed, Costello and Dury emerged as the main attractions, and both engaged in an edgy rivalry to see whose band could provoke the best reactions from the crowds.

In the meantime, events at Stiff's headquarters soon led to a change of label for the singer. Jake Riviera and Dave Robinson had always enjoyed a fiery relationship, and one evening, after one difference of opinion too many, the pair decided it was time to go their separate ways. Robinson assumed sole responsibility for Stiff while Riviera decamped to the newly-founded Radar Records – taking Costello and Nick Lowe with him. This was despite Virgin's Richard Branson coming in with a renewed offer for Costello. A meeting took place but the offer foundered because, when quizzed by Costello, Branson was unable to recall the titles of any of the tracks on *My Aim Is True*, an album he claimed to adore.

While the new arrangements were being finalized Costello and The Attractions jetted out to San Francisco to begin their first US tour. Anticipation had been building Stateside for some while and the tour – culminating in pre-Christmas shows at New York's famous Bottom Line club and New Jersey's Stone Pony (Bruce Springsteen's stamping ground) – helped stir up further interest in *My Aim Is True*.

To round off the tour the band appeared on NBC's influential *Saturday Night Live* TV show (an eleventh-hour substitute for the errant Sex Pistols). Mimicking a great moment in British 1960s TV during which Jimi Hendrix halted a song he was performing live on *The Lulu Show*, Costello ended his version of 'Less Than Zero' after a minute in order to play the acerbic new song, 'Radio Radio'. The song, like its performance, was a typical act of defiance. It was written on the road (from the skeleton of an old Flip City number) as a knee-jerk reaction to the omnipotence of bland AOR radio stations then, as now, dominating US airwaves; as Costello recalls: 'Everywhere you went, you heard the same records... turning the dial there were different parts of the same track on different stations... so, inevitably we took against it.'

Meanwhile, back in the UK Stiff had released the unforgettably spiky 'Watching The Detectives' (recorded at the time of post-Clover auditions, with The Rumour's rhythm section providing the jagged white reggae backing) which bucked the trend set by its predecessors as it made its inexorable way up the UK singles chart. The B-side – featuring live versions of 'Blame It On Cain' and 'Mystery Dance', was the first instance of an 'Elvis Costello and The Attractions' credit.

The end of the year found Costello and the band ensconced with Nick Lowe in London's Eden Studios cutting tracks for a new LP, provisionally titled *The King Of Belgium* (in reference to Costello's striking resemblance to the Low Country monarch, King Albert) and eventually to emerge as *This Year's Model*. With a by now super-drilled band, tanks full of punk-inspired aggression and some of Costello's most tautly written songs on tap, the album couldn't help but promise to build on the approbation and healthy sales afforded its predecessor.

However, the critical acclaim heaped on the album – with Nick Kent calling it 'this joyous event' – was not matched by the spectacular sales that had been forecast. Britain seemed to like it, but it was felt to be a little too acidic for American tastes, as evidenced in the singles 'Pump It Up' and 'I Don't Want To Go To Chelsea' – hits in the UK, nowhere in the US.

This Year's Model was hardly a failure – on commercial or artistic grounds – though the major international breakthrough was still one LP away. Nevertheless, it stands as perhaps the finest example of the new wave pop tendency soon to be practised by the likes of The Pretenders and Squeeze, at once powered by punk yet drawing equally from rock 'n' roll's melodic heritage.

Costello's original intention was to revisit the dirty pop sound of The Rolling Stones' classic *Aftermath* album, and songs like 'Hand In Hand' and 'Little Triggers' certainly seem to quote from the Stones' mid-1960s signature of overloaded amps and bristling melodies. Costello sings and strums with adrenalin-laced brio throughout, and his Larkin-esque gift for wordplay is on acute display ('They call her Natasha when she looks like Elsie – I don't want to go to Chelsea').

But if *This Year's Model* didn't make Costello's name in America, then one of the songs that never made it onto the final cut of the album did. Legendary Country star George Jones had been told about the song 'Stranger In The House' and was persuaded it might make a country-crossover hit. Costello was flown over to Nashville to record the track as a duet with Jones. On his arrival Costello was informed that Jones, a recovering alcoholic, was 'incapacitated'. Costello cut his half of the duet alone and then spent some time soaking up some of the atmosphere of the world's country music capital. It would not be Costello's last foray into country music.

The duet first appeared on Jones' *My Very Special Friends* LP (the other 'friends' included Dolly Parton, Emmylou Harris and Linda Ronstadt, herself later to plunder Costello's oeuvre) and was also included in the first 50,000 copies of *This Year's Model* as a free single backed, for the sake of balance, by a version of The Damned's breakneck anthem, 'Neat Neat Neat'.

In April, Costello and The Attractions were back in Britain touring in support of *This Year's Model*. The highlight of these gigs was undoubtedly an electric version of 'Miracle Man', while Costello's practically a capella take on 'I Just Don't Know What To Do With Myself' prefigures his work with the song's author, Burt Bacharach, by some twenty years. The tour continued to attract critical plaudits and sold-out houses – even though Bruce Thomas was absent with an injured hand. On the tour's final night at London's Roundhouse, Thin Lizzy bassist Phil Lynott handled the encores – themselves something of a rarity.

Despite the personnel problems the UK tour had been a unmitigated success and, in tandem with CBS, Jake Riviera was keen to capitalize on the band's roadworthiness. The next American tour was a marathon, with dates constantly being added as the trek unfurled. It was The Attractions' third Stateside tour in six months. Bruce Thomas recalls how thankful he was for the enforced lay-off provided by his injury. 'The physical workload was pretty devastating. The first couple of years I was at home a handful of nights. Jake went over the top... We'd be in the middle of a 138-day tour, and he'd be wheeling in the gigs for a few months ahead. I'll never forgive him for that.'

Amidst all the hard touring in America, the band still found time to have fun. For The Attractions this meant consuming large amounts of alcohol. Costello was more abstemious, but temptation soon reared its head in another form. Bebe Buell was a fashion model and a former girlfriend of Aerosmith singer Steve Tyler (their daughter Liv is now a Hollywood actress). She met Costello after a 1978 gig at LA's Hollywood High School. The pair began an affair and Costello was soon smitten – bombarding Buell with letters asking her to come back to London with him. The fact that Costello had a wife and child at home seems to have slipped his mind – the constant touring had obviously brought on amnesia.

By an almost Hollywood-style twist of fate Costello and Buell had actually crossed paths some years earlier. In the spring of 1976 she had been modelling for Elizabeth Arden in London when some papers from head office were delivered to the photographic studio. The courier was one Declan MacManus and Buell took an immediate fancy to the blushing messenger boy.

Destiny obviously had more than a fleeting frisson in store.

Having deposited her child with its grandparents, Buell flew to London in August 1978. The pair flaunted their new-found love, and the tabloid press were not slow to report how the new wave singer had abandoned his wife to set up home with Buell in salubrious (and very un-punk) Kensington.

Costello's intense sense of jealousy put paid to the affair within a year (Buell loved the company of musicians, and a wild night at Denny Laine's mansion with punk star Billy Idol – which ended with Buell comatose on a snooker table – was the final straw), and he returned, nominally at least, to the forgiving arms of Mary. When Costello's marriage finally failed in the early 1980s the affair briefly sparked to life again with a series of rendezvous in American motels.

While the Buell affair was waxing and waning, Costello and The Attractions were back in Eden Studios. The album *Armed Forces* (original title: *Emotional Fascism*) was recorded in a relatively luxurious six weeks, with Nick Lowe in the producer's chair. In the meantime, the band squeezed in a mini-tour of Japan and Australasia. Musically, Costello claimed that *Armed Forces* summed up the years of touring and recording which he had so far endured. This was all refracted through a haze of booze (which Costello was now indulging in heavily) and pills, and the band's tour bus listening material: Iggy Pop's *The Idiot*, David Bowie's *Low* and Abba's *Greatest Hits*.

The much-vaunted influence of Iggy Pop and David Bowie is implicit rather than obvious on the album's twelve tracks – though Steve Nieve's battery of keyboards often seem to be regurgitating the whole Abba canon on a single song. This is never more manifest than on 'Oliver's Army', a song originally destined for B-side purdah until Nieve welded on the descending piano riff from 'Dancing Queen' to transform it into a thing of irresistible mellifluousness.

Elsewhere the album hinted at a smorgasbord of 1960s influences: *Abbey Road*-period Beatles invention, updated Booker T and The MGs soul punch, the incandescent symphonic pop of The Beach Boys, Roy Orbison's plangent melodrama and even the chiming baroque of The Byrds. Costello's pun-suffused lyrics melded historical name-dropping (Oliver Cromwell, Adolf Hitler, Mr Churchill) with emblematic archetypes (Party Girls, Big Boys, Busy Bodies), in a Dylanesque cavalcade of lacerating satire – even including himself among the litany of the weak and corrupt in the surely Bebe-inspired 'Accidents Will Happen'.

The album raced into the chart, as did the single 'Oliver's Army', which climbed to UK No. 2.

The success of 'Oliver's Army' changed the scenery for Costello and The Attractions. At a stroke the band/audience hierarchy was altered. 'Before we were all in it together,' Costello muses nostalgically, 'then suddenly this celebrity has been visited on us. You'd play some places and people would look dumbstruck that you were actually there – previously they'd been throwing stuff, gobbing on you, suddenly we were in showbiz. I was ready to pack it in, to be honest.'

Such was the scale of Costello's fame that Riviera began plotting a Beatles-style feature film based around his star's short but meteoric career to date. Perhaps thankfully for all concerned, the idea never got off the drawing board, but its mooting was a genuine reflection of Costello's omnipresence at the close of 1978.

Around the same time, the first of many Elvis impersonators appeared on the scene – sure-fire proof that his image and sound had thoroughly embedded itself in the British pop psyche. Joe Jackson, a lunk of a man squeezed into a Costello-style sharkskin suit, burbled bitterly about his sexual impotence in the hit, 'Is She Really Going Out With Him?', and opened the floodgates for a flotilla of sub-Declan MacManus wannabes parading skinny ties and skinnier songs.

By February, Costello and The Attractions were back in the States. Criss-crossing the continent in a converted Greyhound bus, Costello would restrict his nightly workload to fifty taut minutes, climaxing with a searing version of The Merseybeats' 'I Stand Accused' – a prophetic choice as it transpires. Despite the brevity of the sets and the band's demonstrable road stamina, it wasn't long before fatigue and ill fortune began to creep inexorably into proceedings – compounded by the group's increasing use of cocaine.

In Seattle, the crowd refused to leave the venue, enraged at a forty-minute, encore-less show. The road crew responded by piping screeching white noise into the venue. In Texas, Costello went down with a serious stomach complaint which meant cancelling some engagements. Elsewhere, the band's refusal to grant interviews or do encores would create energy-sapping friction with local press and promoters whose lack of access to the star turn more often than not resulted in barbed reviews. Reporting the tour, *Rolling Stone* described the Costello entourage as, 'A mixture of paranoia and arrogance... By turns petulant and rabid.' That Riviera had the road crew decked out in army fatigues and had a huge sign attached to the tour bus reading 'DESTINATION CAMP LEJEUNE' (the name of a notorious training camp for troops headed for Vietnam) didn't exactly make for a fraternal ambience.

The nadir (of both the tour and, arguably, Costello's career to date), occurred after a show at the Agora club in Columbus, Ohio. The local Holiday Inn happened to be playing host to veteran 1960s singer Stephen Stills and band – at the time the last thing in be-denimed old-wave values. When The Attractions rolled into the lobby that night, still on a mischievous post-gig high, they were almost duty-bound to take exception to the already ensconced older order.

Accepting Stills' convivial offer of a drink in the hotel bar, a seriously inebriated Costello and cohorts then spent an hour winding up the Stills ensemble with a litany of childish provocations. This culminated in Costello decrying all things American, most pointedly music, describing soul superstar James Brown as 'a jive-ass nigger' and the legendary Ray Charles as 'nothing but an ignorant blind nigger'. Stills, much offended by this nasty display of brainless bigotry, shoved Costello off his barstool and retired disgruntled. But this wasn't the end of the incident. Refusing to cease his prejudicial tirade, Costello went on to dismiss Stills' percussionist Joe Lala as a 'greasy spic' and an old fashioned barroom brawl ensued, with Costello being knocked to the ground, dislocating his right shoulder. He later sought to suggest that it took five of Stills' road crew to knock him over, though in fact it was a single blow from feisty blues singer Bonnie Bramlett, then touring with Stills, that ultimately put paid to Costello's devil's advocating.

A gleeful press got hold of the story, which could have seriously damaged Costello's reputation in America. *Armed Forces* was at that moment nestling in the Billboard Top Ten – Columbia's concerted efforts were on the very brink of transforming Costello into a bona fide superstar. Ironically, he had just released a cover version of Nick Lowe's anthemic 'What's So Funny About Peace Love And Understanding?' as an American single.

A panicking CBS rapidly convened a press conference in New York to try and staunch the wound to their charge's reputation, to which Costello was duly summoned. Though apologetic, his vile, thoughtless words had cut deep and the gathered journalists seemed overjoyed at finally cornering him, conspicuously dwelling on *Armed Forces'* ambivalent references to 'white niggers' and 'little Hitlers'. The biter bit, Costello's natural defiance was stirred and any remorse soon got buried under his barely contained rage. The hacks got their story, and Costello's American career would never recover. Ultimately, all those months of not giving interviews had built up a welter of press resentment. Costello was a victim of his own hubris, not to mention stupidity.

Perhaps the ultimate twist of the knife came days later when Ray Charles responded to the incident with a disarmingly dignified even-handedness that contrasted baldly with Costello's impetuousness. 'Anyone could get drunk at least once in his life,' Charles reasoned. 'Drunken talk isn't meant to be printed in the paper, and people should judge Mr Costello by his songs rather than his stupid bar talk.' Touché.

In all the clamour to vilify Costello, no one thought to mention, even by way of irony, that just twelve months earlier he had co-headlined a huge Rock Against Racism concert in London.

With collective tail between legs, Costello and his band completed their tour and returned to the UK. The British music press restricted their comments to the odd snide remark, while the tabloids were more interested in the fact that the singer was seen out and about once again in the company of his wife and child. The late May release and subsequent Top 30 placing of 'Accidents Will Happen' proved that his public had not abandoned him, and that his appetite for music was clearly unaffected by all the peripheral negativity.

When Dave Edmunds took Costello's specially (and rapidly) written 'Girls Talk' (itself another barbed reference to Bebe) into the UK Top 5 in June, his writing abilities seemed to have reached something of a commercial zenith.

In the meantime, Jake Riviera was severing ties with Radar. Contractual problems meant that Riviera had trouble setting up his new F-Beat label, to which Costello and Nick Lowe had both committed. The saga dragged on for almost a year, allowing Costello and the band something like a holiday.

Holiday or not, Costello's muse was visiting again. Inspired by a clutch of Stax, Atlantic and more obscure 1960s soul 45s brought as a £50 job lot from Camden Town's Rock On record emporium, Costello set himself the task of penning songs in the same clipped, punchy style. He also took time out to catch up on the music scene, and produce the debut album of Coventry-based ska act The Specials.

In October, The Attractions and Nick Lowe found themselves in the Dutch provincial town of Wisseloord to record Costello's new soul-influenced songs. The sessions were wild affairs, with Lowe's avowed recording technique of maintaining an air of 'maximum fun' much in evidence.

As the last month of the 1970s dawned, Costello and The Attractions undertook a short southern European tour where they filmed videos for two singles selected from the Dutch recording sessions. Nothing could be released, however, as WEA and F-Beat were still in dispute. The Specials tried to help by releasing Costello's version of Sam and Dave's 'I Can't Stand Up For Falling Down' on their own Two-Tone label. They'd even got as far as manufacturing a few thousand copies before WEA issued a writ, instantly making the singles collectors' gold dust.

Riviera and WEA finally resolved their differences in the early weeks of the new decade, and in March the sardonically-monickered new album *Get Happy!!* was finally unleashed on F-Beat, hot on the heels of 'I Can't Stand Up For Falling Down', now free from WEA house-arrest and a Top 5 hit.

With its weird claustrophobic lyrical themes, Booker T and The MGs groove, and twenty rapid-fire tracks crammed onto a single vinyl LP, *Get Happy!!* was designed to stand out. If nothing else it was bound to put some distance between Costello and a swelling legion of soundalikes. But behind the R&B disguise, some of Costello's old preoccupations were still in evidence. On the almost pomp-rock 'Riot Act', his marriage – or his lack of faith to it – is once again examined, while 'Man Called Uncle' revisits the Bebe affair with renewed self-loathing.

Elsewhere, the lyrics are more obtuse, angular and fragmentary, reflecting Costello's then infatuation with David Bowie's similarly alienated-sounding *Station To Station*, while on doleful tracks like 'Possession', 'Secondary Modern' and 'King Horse', a previously unrevealed tenderness comes achingly to the fore. Even more so on the wistful, waltz-time, 'New Amsterdam'. The elegant Supremes pastiche that is 'High Fidelity', meanwhile, would lodge itself in the mind of writer Nick Hornby so indelibly that he named his best-selling novel after it.

Reaction to *Get Happy!!* was somewhat mixed. *Rolling Stone* called it 'a failure', while *Melody Maker* sought comparisons with Dylan, describing the album, bravely, as 'a *Blood On The Tracks* for the desperate eighties'.

The album, packaged in more of Barney Bubbles' garish geometrics and 'distressed' to resemble a well-thumbed 1960s classic, fared well in charts across Europe – and despite Costello's problems there, the record also sold well in America.

Perversely, however, despite palpable success, the man himself just couldn't get happy. Disillusioned with the music business merry-go-round, Costello even thought about quitting.

He was jerked back to his senses in May when Steve Nieve, vacationing in Los Angeles, was involved in a serious car wreck. 'I realised I was being a bit spoiled,' Costello later admitted, accurately, and he quickly marshalled his resources.

That summer Costello and The Attractions – with a fully recovered Nieve back in harness – played alongside South London band Squeeze at a three-day festival to say goodbye to their departing keyboard player, Jools Holland. One result of these gigs was that Costello struck up a close and lasting friendship with Squeeze's main co-songwriter Chris Difford.

At this time, CBS decided to release a compilation Costello

LP in America, titled *Taking Liberties*. Collating *My Aim Is True* out-takes like 'Doctor Luther's Assistant' and 'Ghost Train', rare B-sides like 'Big Tears' (featuring The Clash's Mick Jones on lead guitar) and Van McCoy's Northern Soul classic 'Getting Mighty Crowded', as well as several alternative takes of LP favourites, the album was an unexpected hit. Originally subject to an import ban in the UK, it was released in the UK on cassette only under the title *Ten Bloody Marys And Ten How's Your Fathers*.

A little stung by some retroactive reviews which preferred the out-takes to the last album proper, Costello and The Attractions entered DJM studios in Holborn, central London, in November 1980 to cut their next LP. Costello's intention was to fuse the rhythmic pulse of *Get Happy!!* with the bristling melodies of *Armed Forces* and to choke back on the direct parodying of 1960s classicism. The session proved fraught – with the Thomases falling out – but fruitful. The Rumour's Martin Belmont and Squeeze's Glenn Tillbrook both contributed to the recordings and helped round out the fuller sound which Nick Lowe was sculpting from the producer's chair. For the first time in their lightning-paced three-year career, the band were actually taking their time.

Perhaps Costello's greatest pun-fest to date, *Trust* is an album of restrained power, fusing some of his oldest 'solo' songs ('New Lace Sleeves' and 'Different Finger' dated back to 1975) with a less Americanized vocal mannerism – perhaps ironically, as his latest obsession was Frank Sinatra. His lyrics were beginning to dwell on the state of the nation – now a good year into the epochal reign of Margaret Thatcher, who would prove to be Costello's nemesis in the years to come. Songs like 'Clubland' and 'Fish 'n' Chip Paper' were overtly political, while sexual politics felt the poison of Costello's pen in 'Big Sister's Clothes' and 'You'll Never Be A Man'.

Whether duetting with a doleful Glenn Tillbrook on 'From A Whisper To A Scream', whooping like a 1950s rockabilly on 'Luxembourg', or throwing out puns like so much confetti on 'Shot With His Own Gun', *Trust* revealed Costello at the very height of his powers. Reviews of the LP were rightly generous, pointing up the seriousness and depth of his songwriting.

However, despite the critical plaudits, trouble might have been right around the corner when the Attractions left England bound for San Francisco in January 1981. It was their first trip to the States since the Ohio hotel incident, and for this reason was christened the English Mugs Tour. Mindful of the privations and attendant lunacy of previous tours, Riviera had booked this latest trip with unusual attention to detail. Gone were the marathon daily drives and weeks without a rest-day; in their place a relatively gentle schedule taking in some of America's most prestigious venues like The Fox Warfield Theatre in San Francisco and Philadelphia's Tower Ballroom. Squeeze, whose *East Side Story* album Costello and Nick Lowe's engineer Roger Bechirian had swiftly co-produced the previous summer, came along as support, which meant there was something close to a family atmosphere on the tour bus.

Riviera's newly adult approach was a clever if expedient managerial decision. There was no way that Costello could return to the States still posing as the irritant upstart – he'd already queered that pitch – and, anyway, his youthful impetuosity was visibly cooling. The more relaxed touring atmosphere only encouraged Costello's apparently convivial mien and a newfound predilection for onstage bonhomie was widely reported.

While America in general was still dubious about Elvis Costello and The Attractions, its musicians proved more than willing to ignore past misdemeanours. Pedal steel virtuoso John McFee joined them for some Southern dates and Texan country-rocker Joe Ely made a cameo appearance in Austin. In Nashville, The

Attractions, with McFee on board, made some tentative record-ings with George Jones' producer Billy Sherrill, paving the way for the *Almost Blue* sessions that would take place later that summer.

When Steve Nieve's girlfriend began experiencing complica-tions related to the birth of the couple's child, the keyboardist was forced to return to London. Even this failed to faze the touring party, with Martin Belmont handling substitute instru-mentalist's duties, and the tour rolled on regardless.

Forgiven, if not forgotten, the Steven Stills incident seemed to be quickly receding from the public debate, and when Costello appeared on an NBC chat show as the very epitome of avun-cular affability, the transformation from pariah to personabili-ty was all but complete. No doubt as a result, *Trust* crept into the US Top 30, and the tour, with Squeeze also receiving press accolades, was pronounced a qualified success. If nothing else, it passed off without controversy, and hopes of a quick restart to Costello's stalled American career were quietly, if over-opti-mistically, harboured.

Back in the UK in March, Costello and The Attractions embarked on a short string of dates – labelled The Tour You Can Trust. Bulkier of physique than in previous incarnations, he no longer seemed interested in attritional posturing but instead appeared rather worldly, peppering his own songs with seamlessly grafted-on snippets from pop classics like Randy Crawford's 'One Day I'll Fly Away' and Bob Marley's 'Jammin''. If, on the surface, this was tantamount to crowd-pleasing – something unthinkable of the taciturn Elvis Costello of twelve months previously – then his refusal to play all but a smattering of the early hits proved that pandering to expecta-tions was still some way off the agenda.

In June Costello was back in Nashville, after reprising his duet with George Jones on a TV special filmed at LA's Country Club. The idea of recording an album of country classics had been at the back of Costello's mind since his first trip to Nashville back in 1978 – possibly longer. It was certainly his intention to put some distance between his twenty-six-year-old self and his various earlier incarnations. 'It's obviously a blessing to have such a powerful image from your first few records, but limiting,' he later professed, admitting, 'The country record was one attempt to escape.'

CBS's Nashville Studio B was the location for the recording of Bob Dylan's epochal 1966 *Blonde On Blonde* album, as well as a host of country hits, and The Attractions approached recording there with due reverence. Unfortunately, when the Costello party arrived Studio B was being renovated and the sessions had to be diverted to Studio A, next door. However, Studio A had also been refurbished and, as Costello recalls, 'it could have been anywhere'. Undaunted, the sessions went ahead with Billy Sherrill in the producer's chair, John McFee at the all-important pedal steel, Tommy Miller on violin and the harmony group Nashville Edition on backing vocals.

It took just two weeks to record and mix the album, though the session was hardly trouble-free: Sherrill thought Costello's choice of songs was old-fashioned (though that was the point), and some of the studio entourage looked askance at these English upstarts daring to record American country classics.

Some of the Nashville studio activity was captured by a documentary film crew making a study of Costello for Britain's *South Bank Show* arts strand. In it, the duelling between Costello and Sherrill takes centre stage, and the whole film is a fascinating document of work-in-progress tensions. The screening of *The South Bank Show* special later that year did much to boost sales of *Almost Blue* in Britain.

Despite the icy atmosphere, the album was completed by early July and the band were invited to help celebrate its completion at the home of country legend Johnny Cash, father of

Carlene Carter, then fiancée of one Nick Lowe. The welcoming bosom of American music was once again being offered in Costello's direction. Similar peace offerings from black artists were, meanwhile, noticeable by their absence.

In July, back in Britain, the band, plus John McFee, played an all-country set at a small club in Aberdeen before a gathered throng of stetson-sporting country and western fans. Ostensibly staged for the benefit of *The South Bank Show*'s cameras, the show also presaged the release of *Almost Blue*, and with several music press reviewers mixing with the rhinestone audience, Costello's 'new direction' was about to be trumpeted to the world.

On its release in October the album befuddled critics. Its maudlin blend of Hank Williams, Charlie Rich and Don Gibson standards was perceived as either a courageous right turn, inconsequential diversion or a misguided folly, often all three in the same review. Costello himself seemed pleased with the diversion and the distance it afforded from the usual music biz circus – a 'controlled corruption', as he described it.

British audiences seemed less perplexed and took to *Almost Blue* with a vengeance. This was aided by the September release of 'A Good Year For The Roses', a misty-eyed, lovelorn ballad written by Jerry Chesnut and once a hit for George Jones. It was Costello's tenderest vocal performance to date, both heartfelt and intimate. It charted in the Top 10 and created a whole new Costello fanbase of sentimental middle-aged women who would accost the singer in the supermarket and treat him, he said, 'like Julio Iglesias'.

In Nashville, as in the rest of the States, the record sunk without trace. The more rock-oriented New Country movement was on the rise, and the last thing the genre needed was an interloping foreigner breezing in with an album of 'they-don't-write-them-like-this-anymore' standards.

All the same, flushed with the relative success of their latest stylistic meander, The Attractions were now attuned to experimentation. After a Christmas lay-off they reunited to essay a comparatively brief world tour through late December and early January, culminating in a one-off show at London's prestigious Royal Albert Hall where they were backed by the full might of The Royal Philharmonic Orchestra. If this latest stunt signalled a return to the crooning style of Ross MacManus then the audience wouldn't have noticed, in the first half of the show at least. Beginning with a handful of *Trust, Get Happy!!* and *Almost Blue* material (pop, soul and country respectively, all held together by the band's controlled aggression), and introducing new songs like the rollicking 'Town Cryer', this was a spirited rock 'n' roll combo in all its pomp. The band seemed relieved to be back to their stripped-down best, even giving the country material an injection of rhythmic pizzazz oddly missing from *Almost Blue*.

'Town Cryer' was just one of a new cache of songs Costello had been steadily penning throughout 1981 – more than enough for a new album. After the *Almost Blue* experience he was keen to take more control of the husbanding of his songs and the bold step to dispense with Nick Lowe's services was taken in late winter 1982 as the band prepared to record in London's Air Studios, run by Beatles producer George Martin.

To help him construct a more architectural studio sound, Costello hired Martin's associate and former Beatles engineer Geoff Emerick, and the sessions, by far the most extensive of Costello's career to date, rolled on into the spring.

The recording dates were an opportunity for the band to contribute more than just their usual efficiently essayed parts and for the first time get involved in the overall creative process. A battery of additional instruments were thrown into the fray, including vibraphone, electric sitar and harpsichord, while extra musicians fleshed out the sound with horns and wood-wind. On 'And In Every Home' a full orchestra was even employed.

As none of the new songs had been ground into submission by a lengthy on-the-road apprenticeship, they were free to develop in wild, often florid directions. The new spirit of artistic endeavour generated by this studio-as-playground approach seemed to bring the band together in a manner rarely possible during the preceding years of frenetic, often fractious, fast-track existence. Even the occasionally tempestuous Bruce Thomas seemed focused on the job and, a first for an Attractions album session, failed to throw his bass at Pete Thomas even once.

Finally christened *Imperial Bedroom* (an attempt, according to Costello, to get 'the right combination of splendour and sleaze') the album was released in June 1982. For the first time Costello allowed the song lyrics to be printed on the inner sleeve (though without punctuation) and Barney Bubbles – after the relative conservatism of *Trust*'s photographic portrait sleeve – went to town, parodying a Cubist Picasso image in his favourite riot of primary colours. David Bailey was commissioned to take the classically posed band shots that adorned the inner sleeve. The accompanying advertising crusade focused on one rhetorical word: 'Masterpiece?'.

Masterpiece or not, the album was certainly a first for Elvis Costello and The Attractions. Exhibiting a melting pot of styles, with songs ebbing and flowing in always intriguing meanders, it finally cut The Attractions loose from any implicit connection to the by now deeply unfashionable pub rock genre. *Imperial Bedroom* begged to be read as art. 'Tears Before Bedtime' was a sophisticated yet naked piece of kitchen sink drama inhabiting a strange sort of metropolitan country music, 'Man Out Of Time' was a churning, Dylanesque portrait of missed opportunities bookended by wild psychedelic wig-outs, while 'Almost Blue', hinting at Cole Porter in the arrangement and Sinatra in the voice, was a bruised, neo-torch ballad.

The English press took to *Imperial Bedroom* with none of the ambivalence shown to *Almost Blue*. Nick Kent, still an unmitigated Costelloite, argued, slightly hysterically, that *Imperial Bedroom* 'should be Number One throughout the charts of the Western World'. The not normally so grandiloquent *Sounds* described Costello as 'Tolstoy among these flea-bitten little rags of half talent'.

Although it reached Number 6 in the UK charts, overall sales of the album were disappointing. In the States, CBS were still hoping for another *Armed Forces* and duly got behind the new record, pushing it into the Top 30 in July. It was the record's peak performance there.

Even though the critics loved *Imperial Bedroom*, Costello seemed somehow to be out of step with the prevailing musical trend of the day. Releasing singles like 'Clubland' that were explicitly antithetical to the new hedonism expounded by louche synth-bands like Spandau Ballet and The Human League didn't do him any favours. Above all else, Costello was still perceived as the worthy if malignant provocateur in the Buddy Holly specs – and as such was hardly likely to fit snugly into a pop scene about to be dominated by Culture Club's androgynous glitz and the deluxe playboy decadence of Duran Duran and Wham. Costello dissected his early 1980s opposition with withering dismissiveness: 'It does happen periodically that you do get a load of people pretending to be homosexuals in shorts.' Miaow.

America was no longer receptive to Costello for different reasons of course. Bad reputations notwithstanding, he and The Attractions undertook yet another US tour in the late summer, presaged by a major interview in *Rolling Stone* with the esteemed 'rock academic' Greil Marcus. In the piece, headlined 'ELVIS COSTELLO REPENTS', the singer tried to lay to rest the ghost of his run-in with Stephen Stills and with it his hateful, vengeful persona of old.

In the autumn the band returned to home shores to essay The Bedrooms Of Britain Tour (secretly billed as The Bail Jake Riviera And F-Beat Out Of The Shit Tour, in reference to the label's latest contractual wrangles) with support from Scottish popsters The Bluebells – whom Costello would later produce.

Late 1982 saw two further releases by Costello and The Attractions. Their somewhat throwaway, brass-saturated contribution to the British movie *Party Party* (the title track, 'written in ten minutes... it sounds like it') was a minor hit single in November, as was a preceding 7" version of Smokey Robinson's 'From Head To Toe' – itself a controversial Jake Riviera scam in which free copies of *Get Happy!!* were given away with the single – but only in 'chart return' shops. A 'controlled corruption' indeed.

In December, English soul siren Dusty Springfield released her *White Heat* album, including Costello's 'Losing You' – a variant on an old song, 'Just A Memory', that he'd written with Springfield in mind. His reverence for 1960s pop classicism was revealed in his excited response to working with Dusty. 'I was actually on the phone, she was transatlantic, singing the new verse, and I've got the phone at arms' length incredulous that I've got Dusty Springfield singing my new verse back to me.'

The beginning of 1983 marked a period of stocktaking. Addressing his disenfranchisement from pop's fast lane – and wondering publicly if the name Elvis Costello wasn't itself now somehow 'jinxed' – Costello had begun writing songs for a new album which, while retaining elements of the old wordiness and musical complexity, were ultimately designed to be nothing short of radio-friendly.

To help him flesh out the new pop direction, Costello had begun cultivating the production team of Clive Langer and Alan Winstanley, then being fêted for their chart-caressing work with Madness, Dexy's Midnight Runners and The Teardrop Explodes, amongst others. With Langer, Costello had written the song 'Shipbuilding' – a poignant protest song about the recently concluded Falklands War between Britain and Argentina, which had been a surprise hit single for Robert Wyatt in September 1982. It remains one of Costello's finest lyrics, a subtly shaded evocation of the reality of war. It did much to enhance Costello's reputation as the most acute political songwriter of his generation and stands as a benchmark against which whole careers (Billy Bragg's or Tracy Chapman's, for example) can be judged. The irony, of course, is that it took the über-pop tunesmith Clive Langer to write the fertile melody.

With Langer and Winstanley, Costello plotted the direction for the new album and, in the meantime, finally did something about that pesky name. In fact his hand was forced. F-Beat's deal with WEA in the UK was about to expire and during the hiatus caused by protracted negotiations between Jake Riviera and RCA for a new distribution deal, Costello went ahead and released a single under the name The Imposter.

Rechristening himself with the title of a *Get Happy!!* track was hardly the densest of smokescreens – it was never intended to be a disguising alias – but losing the Elvis Costello brand certainly did the trick as far as the charts were concerned. 'Pills And Soap' was an odd hit single. Musically inspired by Grandmaster Flash's antediluvian rap 'The Message', this vicious swipe at Margaret Thatcher's ruling Tory party, then about to be reelected for a second term, ruthlessly equated the fate of farm animals with that of a herd-like British electorate. 'Pills And Soap' would prove to be Costello's last Top 20 single for fifteen years.

In the meantime, the album from which it was drawn, *Punch*

The Clock, released in August 1983, was soon scaling the album charts. Langer and Winstanley's leatherette-smooth production had done its job, even if single selections 'Everyday I Write The Book' and 'Let Them All Talk' fared less well than their relentless choruses suggested they might.

With the addition of Dexy's Midnight Runners' brass section (the TKO Horns) and soulful backing vocals from Carol Wheeler and Claudia Fontaine (aka 'Afrodiziak'), *Punch The Clock* was certainly Costello's most accessible album to date. It was also his most plastic. The Attractions seemed to be on autopilot and were rendered anonymous by the homogenizing production gloss. That the adventurous, lo-fi 'Pills And Soap' was the LP's most popular track couldn't have been lost on Costello, for whom *Punch The Clock* had been a transparent attempt at reclaiming his pop star laurels.

In the meantime there was America to consider. With the TKO Horns and Afrodiziak on board, the Clocking In Across America tour unwound through the autumn. The extra musicians revitalized the band's sound and nightly sets included obscure cover versions, everything from Laura Nyro to the O'Jays. With Costello now performing encores in a gorilla suit the old days of rancour and bile seemed like a distant memory – the odd moment of Thatcher-baiting notwithstanding.

America was still proving ill-starred, though. In New York he took to the stage of the Le Parrot nightclub to duet with veteran crooner Tony Bennett backed by the Count Basie Orchestra, as part of a live, televised Bennett gig. A mixture of nerves (Bennett was one of his mother's favourites) and a throat condition rendered Costello's contribution to a version of 'It Don't Mean A Thing (If It Ain't Got That Swing)' hoarse and out of tune. His part was omitted from later reruns.

As the doomy, Orwellian year of 1984 dawned Costello was again addressing his place in the pop firmament. In the middle of drawn-out divorce proceedings from Mary, he recorded what is by some margin his worst album, *Goodbye Cruel World*. Whereas artists like Bob Dylan and Leonard Cohen had turned similar experiences into brilliant 'divorce' albums (Dylan's *Blood On The Tracks* is arguably his finest), Costello found himself up a blind alley. As he told Nick Kent: 'That was a really fucked up record... I had all the arrangements arse-backwards, picked the wrong producers, then asked them to do an impossible job. My marriage was breaking up... it was possibly the worst period of my life.'

By the end of 1984, Costello's febrile attempts to ingratiate himself with the pop mainstream had left his musical integrity in tatters. Recording *Goodbye Cruel World* had been a fraught experience. And it wasn't just the dissolution of his domestic affairs that made 1984 Costello's *annus horribilis*. The Attractions were by now defining the idiom 'familiarity breeds contempt'. They had spent seven intense years inside rock 'n' roll's claustrophobic bubble and were beginning to choke on their own stale air. The reaction to *Goodbye Cruel World* couldn't have helped.

To get away from it all, Costello embarked on a solo tour of America, hiring American singer-songwriter T-Bone Burnett as his support act. Costello and Burnett forged an instant friend-ship based on a mutual regard for American roots music. Joining Costello for nightly encores that rampaged through the country, folk and blues back catalogue, the pair christened themselves 'The Coward Brothers' and acted like long-estranged siblings essaying a homely comeback tour. Costello, observers agreed, suddenly seemed happy.

If the failure of *Goodbye Cruel World* instigated another period of musical dissatisfaction then Costello didn't let it show. He had already produced the anti-apartheid single 'Free Nelson Mandela' for The Special AKA (formerly The Specials) in March, and later in the year assumed the role for the London-Irish folk-punk band The Pogues. Their sophomore album, *Rum, Sodomy And The Lash*, was a critics' favourite and Costello's cachet gained a serious fillip by his association with it. He also gained a new paramour in the lissom shape of Pogues' bassist Cait O'Riordan.

IMP Records also benefited from Costello's lack of other commitments. With Pogues guitarist Phillip Chevron as chief (and only) A&R man, IMP released a series of thoroughly uncommercial singles by the likes of The Men They Couldn't Hang (The Pogues but not as good, essentially), Agnes Bernelle (Weimar cabaret weirdness) and Chevron himself (Brendan Behan songs). All of which helped counterbalance the overt popularism of Costello's last albums.

Which was just as well, as in July RCA issued a TV-advertised Best Of album that served as an unambiguous review of the man's eight-year career to date. At the same time, Costello and T-Bone Burnett released a one-off Coward brothers single, 'The People's Limousine' – a neat country ditty about, naturally enough, Italian Communism – that garnered a fair amount of airplay, if few investors.

On 13 July Costello, sporting a rather folksy beard, played the internationally broadcast charity concert Live Aid, at London's Wembley Stadium. Ever the pop scholar, he chose to sing Lennon and McCartney's 'All You Need Is Love' – itself first unveiled at a similar live, transglobal link-up, back in 1967.

In the autumn he was reunited with The Attractions for one more tour; it would be their last together for a decade. Back home in November they played a Monday night residency at London's Hammersmith Palais – just as The Joe Loss Orchestra used to. Critics noted the blistering pace of the sets and the unrecognizable raggedness of the band.

The latter half of 1985 found Costello in Los Angeles recording a new album with T-Bone Burnett in the producer's chair. The Attractions were scheduled to play on half the tracks on the LP, but in the event only played on one. They were substituted by a retinue of top US session men, including drummer Jim Keltner, bassist Jerry Scheff and guitarist James Burton, all of whom had played in Elvis Presley's 1970s Las Vegas house band. Costello relished working with the new musicians.

'It was like a football team really,' he confirms. 'They stood around while I went through the songs, explaining everything, even my colloquialisms, to ensure that the meanings were clear. I was as honest with them as I could be... They came along with very few prejudices, very open-minded and -hearted. They didn't say "who's this weirdo then?".'

Most tellingly of all, T-Bone Burnett was guiding Costello like no former producer had ever cared, or dared, to. Discouraging him from overwriting (an old fault), Burnett insisted the songs were pared down to their essentials and that the accompanying music should be similarly unelaborate and acoustic-based – in short, folk music.

Burnett's vision and subtlety of approach paid dividends. The album, dubbed *King Of America*, partly in deference to the Elvis connection, was a startling return to form. Confusingly credited to 'The Costello Show Featuring The Attractions And The Confederates', the frontman blurred matters further by going under his full, given name (with the addition of Aloysius, in honour of melancholic English comedian Tony Aloysius Hancock). He appeared on the stark black-and-white cover wearing stubble, a royal crown and, revealingly, a cheeky grin.

The critics were soon swooning over *King Of America*. Old acolyte Nick Kent eulogized; this was a record he urged 'even the most poverty-stricken among you to purchase', while the *Melody Maker* opined, taking a cue from the Declan Patrick Aloysius MacManus credit, that it 'laid the ghost of a defining persona'. Costello explained the retitling to Q magazine, 'The name change is a way to remind people that there was always a human being behind the funny glasses.'

There was special praise for Costello's lyrics, shorn of puns and verbal acrobatics, this was a series of fleeting vignettes, subtle metaphors and cryptic allusions. All very Dylan. All very personal. All very autobiographical.

Then, a mere six months later, Costello reunited with The Attractions to record *Blood And Chocolate*. Setting up in the studio as if for a live performance (and, therefore, ear-splittingly loud), *Blood And Chocolate* proved to be a howling conclusion to a nine-year relationship. Costello, now dubbed Napoleon Dynamite for no explicable reason, wrote the songs in a concentrated burst, pummelling out the backbeat on a tabletop, and, accordingly, a sense of primitive catharsis pervaded the resulting record. Its thunderous drums and cranked-up guitars made *This Year's Model* sound like elevator music.

That Costello's fanbase was back onstream was proven when the merciless racket swaggered into the UK album charts. Released on IMP, the new LP signalled the end of the RCA deal and matters were also coming to a head with Columbia in the States. 'They hated the record,' Costello remembers, 'So I went to them and said, "listen, I don't want to fuck about like this anymore. You tell me the producer, I'll go in with him. I'll fight with anybody, I don't care, with Mutt Lange or any of these guys that were making the big hit records of the mid-'80s. I'll pit my musical personality, voice and strength of will against his, if that's what it takes".' Unsurprisingly Columbia dropped him almost immediately.

But it wasn't all doom and gloom. In May he married Cait O'Riordan in Dublin (a city that would soon become home, partly thanks to Eire's liberal tax arrangements), and in June played the Glastonbury Festival in a pair of comedy trousers.

He was also acting. The odd thespian cameo seemed to be all he was interested in, probably because his acting talents were negligible. Having appeared as a sleazy A&R man in British TV comedy series *The Bullshitters* in 1984, he'd gone on to play an eccentric uncle in Alan Bleasdale's drama *Scully* (for which he penned the workmanlike theme song 'Turning The Town Red') and latterly a bit part – along with The Pogues, The Clash's Joe Strummer and a teenage Courtney Love – in Alex Cox's miserable spaghetti western *Straight To Hell* (for which he and his dad recorded an instrumental, 'A Town Called Big Nothing', MacManus Snr playing trumpet).

1987 saw Costello's musical profile re-established as he undertook tours of America and Europe. Star guests of the calibre of Tom Waits, Tom Petty, The Bangles and Jackson Browne popped up at regular intervals and the shows were ragged marvels, managing to meld gameshow ribaldry with troubadouring gravity and rock 'n' roll thrills.

Most memorable was the twelve-feet-high Spectacular Spinning Songbook, containing the titles of thirty-eight Costello songs, which members of the audience were invited onstage to rotate in order to make the next selection. They were also given the chance to spend the set's duration dancing in a go-go cage.

The 1987 tour haemorrhaged money, but even so *Rolling Stone* critics rated it the year's most successful tour, and they were not alone.

The following year saw Costello ducking below the parapet once more. With no new record on the horizon, Demon issued *Out Of Our Idiot*, another collection of out-takes and rarities. Jake Riviera deigned to speak to the press, revealing that Costello would make another album only 'when he thinks he's got something worth putting out'. It sounded like there might be a long wait.

Writing songs with Paul McCartney might have seemed like 'collaboration' in every sense back in the heady days of punk, but ten years on, Costello's reputation as a premier song crafts-man made him an unusually shrewd choice for the ex-Beatle, then seeking to revitalize his career after years of AOR medi-ocrity and mawkish children's songs.

Costello had first met McCartney at a benefit concert in 1979 and renewed the acquaintance at Air studios during the record-ing of *Imperial Bedroom*, whereupon the older Liverpudlian pronounced himself a fan of the younger.

The songwriting sessions proved profitable to both. McCartney benefited from Costello's unawed approach – a less-er mortal might have baulked at telling the writer of 'Yesterday' and 'Hey Jude' that his melodies weren't up to much. McCartney, for his part, criticized Costello's lack of lyrical nar-rative.

Various press reports suggested that Costello was substituting for John Lennon in an attempt to recapture McCartney's for-mer glories, something that seemed really to irk Costello: 'I hate the way the industry turns people into kind of bubblegum cards or cartoons,' said the man in the giant horn-rims, 'distil-lations of their personality and what they represent, particular-ly in the case of John Lennon... I ain't gonna be involved in any of that crap. It's sentimental nonsense.'

In the summer Costello recorded a new album which includ-ed some of the McCartney-doctored material. Cut in Dublin and New Orleans, *Spike* was an odd confection. With a numer-ous cast list that included McCartney on bass, The Byrds' Roger McGuinn on guitar, Southern soul potentate Allen Toussaint on piano and the Dirty Dozen brass band, it was always going to be a record of disparate sounds and styles. That it maintained an evenness of pace and texture was purely down to the quality of the songs.

Costello's two-year absence from the fray had created a huge sense of anticipation in his still considerable fanbase. On release (by new paymasters Warner Brothers) in February 1989, *Spike* duly shot to Number 5 in the UK chart preceded by the single, 'Veronica' – co-written with McCartney about Costello's elderly aunt – which nudged the Top 30. He was back. Again. As a bonus, the album was a Top 40 hit in America, and *Rolling Stone* named Costello Songwriter of 1989.

And while he'd been away he'd obviously been listening to Tom Waits, particularly his album *Swordfishtrombones*, for much of *Spike* echoes Waits' drunken jazz-junkyard sound. That Waits' sidemen Marc Ribot and Michael Blair appear makes the connection plain. It was a cool reference. As ever, Costello proved he was good at buying records and then remaking them in his own image.

If Costello was tempted to feel good about himself, there was a blot on the landscape. Published in August, Bruce Thomas' *The Big Wheel* was a stinging attack on Costello veiled as an on-the-road journal. In it The Attractions (The Drummer and The Keyboard Player) are depicted as witless fools, drunk and drugged as they traverse the USA in servile thrall to The Singer, whom Thomas dubs Curt Reply and The Pod, amongst other things. It was a witty, cleverly written, if palpably bitter, book that acted as a valve for the years of pent-up frustration Thomas had suffered as The Attractions' 'quiet one'. Costello was wounded by the portrayal, but chose to dismiss the episode with regret that Thomas hadn't enjoyed himself more.

Putting the incident behind him in early 1991, Costello gathered a new set of backing musicians in Barbados to record an LP of cover versions. It was a relaxed two-week schedule, as much a pleasant holiday with new friends as strictly business. All the same the LP, named *Kojak Variety* after a Barbadian department store, would only see the light of day five years later.

Oddly, the *Big Wheel* incident and the conviviality of the *Kojak Variety* sessions didn't spell the end for The Attractions.

Costello had them in mind to record his new album, *Mighty Like A Rose*, but commitments (perhaps imaginary ones in Bruce Thomas' case) meant they were unavailable.

Released in the summer of 1991, *Mighty Like A Rose* carried on where *Spike* had left off. He and Cait had lately become enthralled by classical music and, as he was now composing a score for a new Alan Bleasdale TV series, he began, for the first time, to write musical notation. 'All Grown Up' and 'Harpies Bizarre' from *Mighty Like A Rose* illustrate his élan for the orchestrator's role.

Reviews of the album were mixed. Nevertheless, the LP nearly emulated *Spike*'s success, though it made less headway in the US.

In the meantime, much of Costello's time was taken up by work on the soundtrack to *GBH*, Alan Bleasdale's latest slice-of-life TV drama, in tandem with composer Richard Harvey. The pair later won a BAFTA award for their efforts.

Now seriously smitten with classical music, Costello had become a regular habitué of London's concert halls. He was most taken by a young ensemble called the Brodsky Quartet, who were, in turn, all Costello fans. Soon the two parties were exchanging CDs and telephone numbers. The quartet had already worked with Björk and Paul McCartney, so a 1991 meeting at London's South Bank arts centre in which Costello began sounding them out for a collaboration was not entirely a bolt from the blue.

Inspiration for the album Costello and the Brodskys would work on throughout 1992 came initially from Cait O'Riordan. She had kept a newspaper cutting concerning a Veronese academic who had taken it upon himself to answer all letters sent to the fictional Juliet Capulet (the 'female lead' in Shakespeare's *Romeo And Juliet*). Costello quickly became obsessed by the article and was soon charting a song cycle based on a similarly unconnected string of epistles.

The Juliet Letters, released in January 1993 and a surprise hit in the UK, presented an Elvis Costello light years removed from any former incarnation. With the Brodskys handling the chamber music backing and a guitarless Costello the letter-themed libretto, this was as stark an antithesis to rock 'n' roll as could be imagined. In places it worked, Costello's singing, though hardly operatic, glided amongst the sonorous strings with confident ease. Occasionally pretension got the better of him and the slow vibrato he'd learned during recent formal singing lessons sounded false and contrived whenever he overused it, which was quite often.

Though very little now seemed impossible for the versatile Costello, his next jaunt still came as a major surprise. Peroxide pop singer Wendy James of late 1980s British cartoon rockers Transvision Vamp was an unlikely muse for the man who'd lately listed Shostakovich as his favourite artist.

James, a tiny, self-publicizing clotheshorse with an irritating squeak of a voice and a penchant for meaningless sloganeering posing as lyrics, had lately fallen on hard times. Her once chart-hogging combo were on the skids and she was now desperate for some credibility or, at the very least, a way back in to the pop corpus.

After a chance meeting with Pete Thomas she was persuaded to pen a missive to Costello – of whom she'd been a long-time fan – seeking advice. What she got, after a two week-wait during which she'd given up on the whole affair, was an album's-worth of brand-new Costello songs, called *Now Ain't The Time For Your Tears* – which promptly sank without trace.

But there were benefits for Costello. Writing an album of old-fashioned rock songs, on which he worked with Pete Thomas, led him to think of re-forming The Attractions. In a mid-1993 rush he penned a slew of new songs that just begged for his old combo to get their chops around. Pete Thomas was available and Steve Nieve was prised away from session work with soul veteran Sam Moore (and a lucrative sideline in advertising jingles). Only the bassist's role remained a stumbling block.

Initially overcoming the problem by welcoming Nick Lowe back into the fold (the new ensemble being briefly re-christened 'The Distractions'), early sessions proved his bass-playing abilities to be limited on the more complex numbers, and finally Costello extended an olive branch and summoned Bruce Thomas from exile in proverbial Siberia.

Any lingering intra-band animosity soon got buried by the fun and intensity of work. Excited rumours did the rounds of the music press to the effect that the new record would be a bona fide Elvis Costello and The Attractions effort. It was, but for reasons unstated (possibly because Nick Lowe eventually played bass on almost half the numbers) the record was credited only to the leader.

Brutal Youth appeared in March 1994 to general plaudits. It was a hit in the UK, as was the single 'Sulky Girl'. The LP also charted in the US – to the delight of Warner Brothers, who booked the band onto *The Letterman Show* and generally put their weight behind this eminently saleable commodity.

Seizing the cudgel, the band were soon back on the road, a seven-month world tour that combined a greatest hits review with promotion of the new album. Though there were inevitable niggles, The Attractions seemed to have lost none of their power, even if their alcohol intake was not what it was (Costello had forsworn the drink totally, confessing that he'd 'lost the taste for it').

In September Costello's eighteen-year relationship with Jake Riviera ended. The world's tour promoters breathed a collective sigh of relief and Costello formed his own management company, By Eleven.

1995 was business as usual for renaissance man Costello. At

the year's beginning he was out on the road in the guise of a folk troubadour, supporting his old hero Bob Dylan on the latest European leg of the man's eternal world tour. He even got to duet with the master during the encores.

In May, *Kojak Variety* was finally released – to little acclaim. Then there was his contribution to *Weird Nightmare*, an eccentric tribute to jazz legend Charles Mingus, a classical piece written for a celebration of seventeenth-century English composer Henry Purcell, and an odd re-visitation of old songs, *Deep Dead Blue*, a mini-album recorded live with guitarist Bill Frisell at London's Meltdown Festival, for which Costello was that year's guest curator.

And there was more. With Paul McCartney and The Brodsky Quartet he played a private concert for Prince Charles and gathered dignitaries at St James's Palace in June; socialist Costello not so much taking the King's shilling as extracting it – this all being in aid of charity, he was quick to point out.

Back in Dublin he composed *Three Distracted Women* for The Brodsky Quartet and German soprano Anne Sofie von Otter, then sang songs from Shakespeare's *Twelfth Night* live with saxophonist John Harle. Also in November he received *Q* magazine's Best Songwriter award to go with the Ivor Novello award for Most Outstanding Contemporary Song Collection he had snaffled in May. He also began gathering songs for a new album.

All This Useless Beauty was a collection of songs Costello had written for other artists over the years. The original idea was to release the tracks, one a month, throughout the year. This got toned down to four singles in a month, to the chagrin of Warner Brothers who, correctly, saw this as self-indulgent folly. No one bought the records anyway, despite guest 'extra track' appearances from hip young artists like Tricky and Sleeper.

Before the album was released, Costello undertook a US tour

with Steve Nieve as his only backing. It was a surprisingly successful formula, Nieve's one-man orchestra of keyboards given full rein in service of Costello's mighty repertoire. Later dates with The Attractions ensemble were riven with fatigue and ill-feeling. By the closing Japanese dates Bruce Thomas wasn't talking to the boss again, and after a sayonara in Nagoya the band dispersed, probably for ever.

All This Useless Beauty received a lukewarm reception and once again Costello found himself itching for a new way of expressing himself, some new inspiration – which arrived in the form of easy listening legend Burt Bacharach.

Costello had first encountered Bacharach during the recording of *Spike,* and the two had remained vaguely in touch. Their friendship resulted in a co-composition, 'God Give Me Strength', which was written by fax and telephone. The song, which appeared on the soundtrack to the 1997 feature film *Grace Of My Heart*, was a sublime melding of Bacharach's lilting orchestral pop arrangements and Costello's keening melodies.

Like his earlier collaborations with Paul McCartney, there was a neat symbiosis in the pairing of Costello with the silver-haired Californian lounge-meister. The mature Elvis Costello was by now a musician of catholic but refined tastes, equally at home with a madrigal as he was a torch song or a country-rocker. Likewise Bacharach, the co-composer of some of the western world's best loved pop standards, could turn his hand to a range of styles – though always leaving his silkily euphonious signature on the end result. As Costello remarked at the time, 'It's hard to get past who Bacharach is, but he's a very easy-going chap. He's a thorough musician but not a muso... he's got everything.'

Bacharach repaid the compliment, saying of Costello, 'I knew where he was coming from... I think he wasn't just into my music, he was in to all music.'

With Costello now signed to a worldwide deal with Mercury/Universal, an album of Bacharach/Costello compositions, *Painted From Memory*, was recorded in Los Angeles with a full orchestra, backing vocalists and Steve Nieve on various keyboards. It was a somewhat studious affair, an exercise in lightweight sophistication, but it had its moments.

The post-Bacharach period has been a strange one for Elvis Costello. In 1999 his new label Universal issued yet another greatest hits collection, *The Very Best Of...* (with tracks cherry-picked by Costello himself), which included his version of the Charles Aznavour song, 'She'. Included in the hit film *Notting Hill*, 'She' became Costello's biggest hit since 'Oliver's Army'.

The late 1990s also saw a welter of CD reissues – all Costello's major albums reappeared with extra tracks and insightful, and occasionally tongue-in-cheek, notes from the man himself.

In 1998 he answered questions posed by readers of *Q* Magazine in which he nixed the idea of future Attractions records; 'there's bad blood', he admitted, candidly. Two Costello records appeared in the same magazine's list of the 100 Greatest British Albums, published in June 2000: *This Year's Model* at 84 and *Armed Forces* at 45, the latter lodged between The Smiths and Pulp.

What Elvis Costello does next is anyone's guess. His has become the most unpredictable, not to mention enduring, odyssey. While his class of 1977 peers have generally seen their careers wilt or stagger into self-parody (or cease altogether, only to re-emerge in a litany of credibility-denting, if lucrative, reunions), Costello has never faltered. Not all of his creative decisions along the way have been brilliant, but his dominant drive remains one of self-challenge, and he is still looking to broaden his scope. These are rare and extremely laudable characteristics. Like Tom Waits (and few others), he has been brave enough to make his most experimental work as he enters middle age, while at the same time exhibiting the musical wisdom and acuity of a man at ease with his place in a shady corner of rock's pantheon.

In a 1996 interview Costello put forward the possibility of deleting his entire back catalogue at the turn of the millennium and taking off on an untried course. So far nothing has gone out of print. The clever money, however, must still be on that new adventure.

TWO

THE MUSIC

My Aim Is True

Label: Stiff
Released: July 1977
Chart Position: UK: 14, US: 32
Producer: Nick Lowe
Engineer: Uncredited
Recorded: October 1976, Pathway Studio, London

> *Costello's debut LP fused the angst of punk with the musicality of pub rock. Backing group Clover (billed as 'The Shamrocks') turn in a sympathetic if slightly dainty performance, while Lowe's cardboard production does nobody any favours. Somehow it continues to sound classic.*

Welcome To The Working Week

Clipped, and at times frenzied, mutant R&B. At well under two minutes it was an explosive opening gambit. Costello's voice is an exact amalgam of Van Morrison, Graham Parker and Jesse Winchester, though the urgency of delivery is all his own.

Miracle Man

The impotent (in every sense) male is a subject to which this album continually returns, with this the most unremitting example. John McFee unwinds a string of sub-Keith Richards guitar licks around Costello's impassioned vocal which, for all its ferocity, appears to have been recorded in a shoebox. Exhilarating all the same.

No Dancing

Melodically akin to The Ronettes' 'Be My Baby'. More libidinous frustration, more exciting ensemble rocking, with Costello sounding genuinely exasperated by the close. 'Dancing', for the uninitiated, is Costelloian for sex.

Blame It On Cain

Southern R&B re-tooled for punk London. Breezy and possessed of a mighty chorus, it invokes the son of Adam in a sardonic treatise on unquenchable urges: 'It's nobody's fault, but it just seems to be his turn', goes the wryly mocking chorus pay-off.

Alison

Never as gorgeous here as in various later, live versions with The Attractions, this is still the most aching-yet-knowing evocation of unrequited love. Inventive lead guitar snakes around Costello's wonderfully hurt vocal, one minute chiding, the next soothing, while the chorus plea provides not only the name of the LP but Costello's artistic *cri de coeur*. As serene and heartbroken a torch ballad as the man will ever write.

Sneaky Feelings

Randy Newman on steroids. Costello sounds petulant and mannered in this bitter, vengeful little essay. The band, meanwhile, are taut and controlled – though their country fills and backing 'oohs' are strictly old-wave.

(The Angels Wanna Wear My) Red Shoes

Kicking off with Byrds-like guitar shimmer and Costello's pithy axiom: 'I used to be disgusted, but now I try to be amused', this is another memorably urgent slab of new wave rock, with a pugnacious vocal that sounds a good deal more like Graham Parker than it does Declan MacManus. Terrific, for all that.

Less Than Zero

A reprise for Costello's debut single – a feisty, lo-fi calling card. Name-checking notorious English 1930s fascist Oswald Mosley, Costello muses wittily about existential futility while the band play a trebly hybrid of ska and garage punk. The 'hey-wahey' chorus is very much of its time.

Mystery Dance

A pounding Doctor Feelgood facsimile. Straight-ahead, high-velocity R&B in other words, framing more of Costello's pent-up, adolescent appetites in another extended euphemism for the taboos surrounding sexual congress. Suitably, the song is all over in a couple of minutes. Great while it lasts, though.

Pay It Back

This dates back to Flip City days – and it shows. Tinny soul riffing, jaunty piano, a preposterously Americanized vocal lilt and the dullest of tunes make for the album's low point.

I'm Not Angry

This could be The Only Ones or even Spooky Tooth, such is the tensile ambience of its sinuous intro, with John McFee's careening guitar pulling the band into some impressive rock shapes while a mordant Costello does his best to disprove the song's title.

Waiting For The End Of The World

Grinding rock 'n' roll, replete with slide guitar and an irascible

Costello coming over all apocalyptic as he's stuck between stations on the London Underground. Even his swaggering sub-Jagger drawl can't arrest the ineffable sense of ennui that pervades this otherwise rollicking finale.

Watching The Detectives

An extra track on the US version. A stream of brilliantly evoked cinematic images ('She's filing her nails while they're dragging the lake …') and a nervy, twitching reggae backbeat distinguish this sophisticated exercise in pop noir. It also contains some of Costello's finest twanging tremolo guitar work. A Number 15 hit single in the UK.

This Year's Model

Label:	Radar (UK), Columbia (US)
Released:	March 1978
Chart Position:	UK: 4, US: 3
Producer:	Nick Lowe
Engineer:	Uncredited
Recorded:	January 1978, Eden Studios, London

The album that reaffirmed an angsty reputation. With The Attractions now on board, Costello lays waste to early Rolling Stones-style raunch with a torrent of lyrical invective and some of the most splendidly cack-handed rhythm guitar playing ever to grace the charts. It has dated a tad, but the visceral thrills remain.

No Action

An extended telecommunication pun ('every time I phone you I just want to put you down') set to a pumping neo-beat group backing. The Attractions say a vigorous 'hello', though for the only time on record Steve Nieve's keyboards are all but inaudible beneath Costello's crunching guitar chords.

This Year's Girl

With staccato drum rhythms, lugubrious bass and a keyboard riff that is possibly a tongue-in-cheek tribute to Gary Numan, this withering attack on fashion and superficiality proved The Attractions' élan with a more subtle musical canvas. Costello's double-tracked vocals are one big musical sneer.

The Beat

Soulful guitar riffing – reminiscent of The Rumour – leads into this disdainful, keyboard-soaked paean to onanism ('I don't wanna be your lover, I just wanna be your victim'). The chorus is a dead ringer for mid-'60s Kinks.

Pump It Up

Bob Dylan's 'Subterranean Homesick Blues' remade for the accelerating 1970s. A huge, bruising Pete Thomas beat and a chorus of laconic anthemicism continue to render this as vital and undeniable a rocker as the Costello oeuvre contains. The author hits his guitar so hard it goes horribly out of tune towards the close. The result sounds great.

Little Triggers

A respite, this is country soul with a touch of Burt Bacharach in the verse, barely withheld malice on the choruses. Nieve's piano makes an elegant counterpoint to Costello's choked vocal. A song about verbal put-downs sung in verbal acrobatese.

You Belong To Me

Redolent of The Rolling Stones' 'The Last Time' (though Bruce Thomas appears to be playing 'Nineteenth Nervous Breakdown') this is the nearest Costello gets to emulating Jagger and co's *Aftermath* LP – his avowed intention on *This Year's Model*. Another stinging chorus, more romantic desperation and a guitar sound like a shower of iron filings all feature.

Hand In Hand

Starts with a Beatles-like backwards vocal effect before seguing into a mid-paced rocker about doomed love (what else?). The Attractions are on autopilot, but the chorus is nagging. Costello's twelve-string overdub, meanwhile, is plain annoying.

(I Don't Want To Go To) Chelsea

A rakish melding of kitsch 1960s riffing, indolent vocals and lyrics set in a lost 'swinging London' that take a machete to the aspirations of the English middle classes, this is as jauntily melodic as it is splenetic. Within a year of penning it Costello would have taken up residence in the Royal Borough of Kensington and Chelsea. Go figure.

Lip Service

Despite a lyric that posits oral sex as an emblem of subservience, this still tries hard to be a banal little pop song. The distinctly Graham Parker-esque chorus almost rescues it. 'Going through the motions', indeed.

Living In Paradise

Sexual jealousy and the phenomenon of America conjoined in a strangely vulnerable lyric ('You're already looking for another fool like me'). Costello plays some neat Steve Cropper-esque guitar fills, while his fulminating, multi-tracked vocals hint at later studio manipulations.

Lipstick Vogue

A complex song, with multiple time changes, a lengthy instrumental bridge and a chorus worthy of *Blonde On Blonde*-era Dylan. Costello is a deeply disenfranchised narrator railing against his alienation while the band play fast and loose with a churning backing, all to memorable effect.

Night Rally

A dark, Orwellian vision of the future set to a plangent backing reminiscent of Procul Harum. Steve Nieve is the star, his chilling organ notes piercing the atmospheric grandeur as Costello's paranoiac totalitarian prophecy unfurls. Genuinely scary.

Radio Radio

Added to the US version. Costello at his angriest, railing against the crippling homogenization of American culture. The Attractions go for broke — rendering the song as a sort of sped-up '(I Can't Get No) Satisfaction'. Blunt but thrilling.

Armed Forces

Label:	Radar (UK), Columbia (US)
Released:	January 1979
Chart position:	UK: 2, US: 10
Producer:	Nick Lowe
Engineer:	Uncredited
Recorded:	October 1978, Eden Studios, London

The album that made Elvis Costello, briefly, a global superstar. Regiments of military metaphors, torrents of sub-Wildean puns and a shimmering confection of rock, pop and soul styles make for the man's most fully realized 1970s album.

Accidents Will Happen

An elegantly unwinding treatise on temptation in which Costello drily addresses his new-found attractiveness to members of the opposite sex. Eschewing the bitterness of yore, he sounds almost resigned as the band uncoil a serpentine backing that recalls the *Abbey Road*-period Beatles. Sophisticated adult pop music de luxe.

Senior Service

The hierarchy of the workplace is an unusual subject for a pop song. The Attractions give it a suitably off-kilter treatment, Nieve's jagged Vox Continental organ to the fore – none of which interrupts the positively chirruping vocal melody or witty wordplay ('it's a death that's worse than fate').

Oliver's Army

The kind of descending piano cascade that punctuates Abba's 'Dancing Queen' transforms a pedestrian power-pop rant (about mercenaries and the last days of colonial empire) into a thing of chiming, symphonic euphoria. Still Costello's best-loved song, its unexpected, career-eclipsing success as a single nearly finished him off. Notoriously difficult to hear without singing along.

Big Boys

Droning synthesizers create a sinister atmosphere and the bass, soaked in reverb, tries valiantly to make this Costello-by-numbers makeweight sound edgy. It fails, as does the song, beautifully played and sung though it is.

Green Shirt

This is authentically odd. Harpsichord and Georgio Moroder-aping sequencer underpin another paranoid vision of futuristic government control intertwined with a moral-free sexual realpolitik. Eerie and cinematic of lyric ('You better cut off all identifying labels, before they put you onto the torture table') it's thoroughly unsettling, despite the most mellifluous contributions from Bruce Thomas' unfettered bass. A unique conflation of fear and joy.

Party Girl

'Alison' revisited. This time her name is, quite conceivably, Bebe. More exquisite bass dolefulness from Bruce Thomas propels this stately, lovelorn ballad with Costello in fine, intimate voice. The closing 'I could give you anything but time' mantra sounds like another *Abbey Road* out-take. Wonderfully dynamic.

Goon Squad

A raunchy intro – the voluptuous guitar could almost be Duane Eddy – segues into a pulsating, up-tempo rock song. Bruce Thomas bends his bass into more unfathomable configurations as Costello whines feverishly about military subterfuge from the viewpoint of a raw recruit. A 'goon squad' is army jargon for a band of mercenaries; parallels with the perma-touring Attractions are implicit but obvious.

Busy Bodies

A pun-fest set to more pumping neo-R&B. The guitar riff is from the school of Booker T and The MGs and the final vocal refrain from the Beach Boys. If you're going to steal you might as well do it from the best. Costello proves himself the most judicious of magpies.

Sunday's Best

Jerky fairground organ and circus drums recall The Kinks' cod-vaude-villian departures (and thus Madness and Blur) – all of which is appropriate to an arch song about tabloid newspapers and English small-mindedness, wherein the hapless populace are depicted as 'at death's door with life assurance'. Scabrous.

Moods For Moderns

More Booker T stylings overlaid with a chorus redolent of The Beatles' *Rubber Soul*. A perfunctory ditty about disaffected youth, it is principally notable for Costello's muted but rather fine attempt at a guitar solo on the coda.

Chemistry Class

A song with few parallels. Baroque and richly melodic, the gorgeous backing even ameliorates Costello's contentious query, 'Are you ready for the final solution?' – which somehow equates the Holocaust with the failing 'chemistry' of a relationship. Lyrical 'audacity' notwithstanding, this is fabulous.

Two Little Hitlers

The Nazi theme again intrudes. 'Little Hitler' was a working title for Costello's second album, which Nick Lowe subsequently purloined for a song of his own. Hence the title here. Overburdened with textual gymnastics ('she's so calculating, she's got a calculator') and a meagre tune, it is superfluous here – despite the chorus's nod to David Bowie's 'Rebel Rebel'.

(What's So Funny 'Bout) Peace Love And Understanding

Originally the B-side to Nick Lowe's 'American Squirm' single, this helped rocket *Armed Forces* into the US Top 10 by inclusion on the LP's Stateside version (at the expense of the parochial 'Sunday's Best'). A joyous anthem to Woodstock values, it held less water in cynical, post-punk Britain. A genuine 1970s classic with a regal chord progression and hymnal melody worthy of prime Bruce Springsteen, for all that.

Get Happy!!

Label:	F-Beat (UK), Columbia (US)
Released:	February 1980
Chart position:	UK: 2, US: 11
Producer:	Nick Lowe
Engineer:	Uncredited
Recorded:	October 1979, Wisseloord Studios, Holland

The finest example of Costello as ace pasticheur. Remoulding classic soul 45s into oddly futuristic-sounding pop, Get Happy!!'s *twenty tracks were crammed onto two sides of vinyl like a greatest hits package from a parallel universe.*

Love For Tender

Melodically, a Supremes song in all but name, this is also a decidedly un-Motown-like, misbegotten stream of loveless images. The band punctuate Costello's bruised, alienated lyric with a shuffling rhythm and opaque instrumentation. It's all over, seemingly, seconds after it begins.

Opportunity

Costello's vocals are all but inaudible, but his Curtis Mayfield-style guitar is upfront, along with Nieve's bubbling Hammond organ. The descending chorus chords suggest soul euphoria but the song is actually about surveillance ('whatever you do, don't turn around') – a paranoid mood certainly pervades.

The Imposter

Too fast for soul, too slippery for punk, this really is a unique pop hybrid. A chilling lyric about falling short of expectations and some unctuous fairground organ maintain the album's undertone of eerie 'otherness'.

Secondary Modern

Romance, sex and lost innocence ('Is it pleasure or business, or a packet of three?') set to an airtight soul groove. Costello seems detached – the casual observer at the teenage party. A nostalgic glance back to a Birkenhead adolescence.

Possession

A chord sequence seemingly plucked from the Lennon and McCartney songbook and an organ riff from heaven distinguish this alluring pop construction. Costello ruins it with overwrought lyrical gymnastics ('you lack lust, you're so lacklustre'). A song about the malignancy of money.

Man Called Uncle

Another oblique reference to the Buell affair ('other girls I see just leave me cold') and a biting return to an old concern – male impotence. Costello sounds embittered and at the end of his tether – despite a cushion of Lowe's most luxuriant reverb. Pete Thomas' snare drum sounds like a Gatling gun.

Clowntime Is Over

An alluring melody and a terrific, understated performance from The Attractions. In the most intimate vocal on the record, Costello paints himself as 'a voice in the shadows' about to get down to some serious (presumably musical) work. His avowal to 'make Lovers' Lane safe for lovers again', sounds a more daunting prospect.

New Amsterdam

An emotional travelogue set to a waltz-time rhythm, reminiscent of The Beatles' 'You've Got To Hide Your Love Away'. A seductive blend of acoustic guitars and a sublime vocal melody usher us down memory lane. Name-checking Liverpool and London, this is a honey-coated portrait of existential rootlessness ('Although I look right at home I still feel like an exile'). Costello plays most of the instruments himself – it's one of his finest recorded moments.

High Fidelity

More soulful, bucolic funk from the band, more hoarse pleading about faithlessness from Costello. There's genuine torture in the voice here – and a sublime organ coda from Nieve. A non-hit as a single despite a chorus melody straight out of the Holland-Dozier-Holland Motown finishing school.

I Can't Stand Up For Falling Down

A lesser known Sam 'n' Dave cover introduces the old vinyl album's second side on a brisk, finger-popping note. A hit as a single, its rumbustious chorus defines the term nagging.

Black And White World

Compressed and suffocating in atmosphere, this is edgy and myste-rious, with a dense lyric possibly about the duplicity of the Press. Choppy organ and a rapid-fire guitar solo provide the all-too-brief respite.

Five Gears In Reverse

The bass is mixed louder than the voice – just like a classic Stax record – and Bruce Thomas is on his funkiest behaviour. The lyrics, when you can discern them, seem to be dwelling on human frailties. Intriguing.

B-Movie

More choice grooves – both Thomas' *in excelcis* – underscore another crisp reworking of the Booker T prototype. The whole thing seems to be suspended in space courtesy of Lowe's weirdly applied echo. Possibly a curt dismissal of Bebe Buell ('B-Movie, that's all you're to me').

Motel Matches

Perhaps the album's finest song. The tone and structure of 'Alison' reworked into a yearning, crestfallen ballad. Puns abound ('I struck lucky with Motel Matches') and Nieve's piano and organ work recall The Band's Garth Hudson. Again, it's difficult to imagine this not being about Bebe Buell. Bruised but lovely.

Human Touch

Junkshop ska – Prince Buster via Mars. Costello sounds wracked with pain as he intones about an elusive lover who 'looks like a luxury, feels like a disease'. Not nice, but oddly compelling.

Beaten To The Punch

Tinny but rocking – like an ancient soul record heard on a cheap transistor radio. More desperation from Costello, deft swaggering from the band. The 'Mr Punch' impersonation at the close is terrifying.

Temptation

A song that was allegedly written around the riff to Booker T's 'Time Is Tight'. This time the singer floats in a lake of echo and pleads as if from the bowels of the earth for someone to 'give me temptation'. The band, of course, could have played 'Time Is Tight' in their sleep.

I Stand Accused

The Merseybeats' 1960s stomper taken at a rate of knots, with Bruce Thomas apparently playing 'Flight Of The Bumble Bee' simultaneously. The Attractions ooze power and dexterity in equal measure. Costello sounds like a man sweating on the witness stand and his throwaway harmonica solo is perfect.

Riot Act

Oddly recorded (the drums are gated out of existence) this lolloping ballad sounds like Procul Harum after a bad trip. Nieve's keyboards are quite mad and the chorus sumptuous. Costello's voice is all but shot which makes him that bit more believable, and the song staggers off on an opulent coda filleted by Bruce Thomas' McCartney-esque bass. Draining but brilliant.

Taking Liberties (US)/Ten Bloody Marys and Ten How's Your Fathers (UK)

Label:	F-Beat (UK), Columbia (US)
Released:	October/November 1980
Chart Position:	UK: 28, US: did not chart
Producers:	Nick Lowe, Elvis Costello
Engineers:	Various
Recorded:	Between 1976 and 1980, in various locations

B-sides and rarities collection that was early proof of Costello's protean versatility. The UK version was originally issued in cassette form only, gaining a full release in 1984.

Clean Money
The Attractions in driving form on this abrasive, if rather tuneless, *Trust* out-take.

Girls Talk
A hit for Dave Edmunds, here in equally mellifluous form courtesy of Costello and the band in their *Armed Forces*-era pomp.

Talking In The Dark
Left off *Armed Forces* but full of that album's claustrophobia and musical invention.

Radio Sweetheart
B-side of the debut single. Clover play like an adept American bar band, unsurprisingly.

Black And White World
Twitchy alternative to the *Get Happy!!* version with Costello showing off his considerable vocal range.

Big Tears
An upset, minor-key anthem with The Clash's Mick Jones on winsome lead guitar. The B-side to 'Pump It Up'.

Just A Memory
Classic, lovelorn songwriting with a bitter twist. This would have graced any of the first four albums, but didn't. From the initial, abortive *Get Happy!!* sessions.

Night Rally
Left off the US version of *This Year's Model*.

Stranger In The House
The 1978 George Jones duet salvaged from Stiff promo obscurity. Jones' ancient croak and Costello's coolly restrained delivery blend startlingly well. Aching.

Clowntime Is Over
Alternative version of *The Get Happy!!* standout. Very much The Attractions-by-numbers, this lacks the intimacy of the album take.

Getting Mighty Crowded
Van McCoy's Northern Soul standard given the full *Get Happy!!* treatment. Originally the B-side to 'High Fidelity'.

Hoover Factory
From the first *My Aim Is True* sessions, with Costello and Clover sculpting a surprisingly sophisticated baroque setting for this homage to a landmark Art Deco building in west London.

Tiny Steps
Likeable if ultimately lightweight out-take from *This Year's Model*. The B-side of 'Radio Radio' in the UK.

(I Don't Want To Go To) Chelsea
A hit single in the UK but inexplicably unreleased before this in the US.

Dr Luther's Assistant
Obscure and arcane lyrics and another intimate 1976 studio performance from Clover. It remained unreleased for over three years because Costello would have risked 'showing that I knew more than three chords'.

Sunday's Best
Omitted from the US version of *Armed Forces*.

(What's So Funny 'Bout) Peace Love And Understanding
Previously omitted from the UK album.

Crawling To The USA
Workmanlike song from the soundtrack to the US feature film *Americathon*.

Wednesday Week
Wistful *Armed Forces* refugee. Could have used a more robust tune.

My Funny Valentine

Excellent reading of the Rodgers and Hart classic, with Costello sounding like Chet Baker while accompanying himself on jazzy guitar. The B-side to 'Oliver's Army'.

Ghost Train

Clover show off their chops on this terrific *My Aim Is True* off-cut. Mildly impenetrable lyrics but a great, angst-free vocal from Costello.

Trust

Label:	F-Beat (UK), Columbia (US)
Released:	January 1981
Chart position:	UK: 9, US: 28
Producer:	Nick Lowe
Engineer:	Roger Bechirian
Recorded:	November 1980, DJM and Eden Studios, London

Costello's fifth album-proper in less than four years was a consolidation of, rather than expansion upon, his oeuvre to date. A lack of chart-worrying singles has allowed it to drift into relative obscurity.

Clubland

If nothing else, *Trust* represents the very apex of Costello's fixation with puns and 'Clubland' is perhaps its very apogee ('have you ever been had, in Clubland?'). Sung to a taut piano-dappled 1960s groove, this is an uncompromising essay on working-class escapism. The testy, bark-along chorus deserves to have made it a hit, but didn't.

Lovers Walk

A song predicated on Bo Diddley's trademark shuffle beat, given extra emphasis by Pete Thomas' resounding tom-toms. Costello sings with a paranoiac's edge ('be on caution when lovers walk') while Nieve revisits The Champs' 'Tequila' on the tinkling ivories. Worthy.

You'll Never Be A Man

Pete Thomas again to the fore in this soulful analysis of sexual failure. The band are watertight but the musical moves are entirely predictable. Less than the sum of its parts.

Pretty Words

Obtuse and labyrinthine in the lyrics (a shamed lover figures, as he/she does on much of *Trust*) and decked out in Nieve's most glittering arpeggios, the song nevertheless fails ever to get going.

Strict Time

Buttoned-up suburban dating and mating rituals given the full pun treatment ('more like a hand-job than a hand-jive'). A pedestrian twelve-bar blues lurks uncomfortably beneath the Thomases' rhythmic invention.

Luxembourg

Elvis-does-Elvis. A rockabilly stomp that appears to have little to do with the northern European principality. The Rumour's Martin Belmont plays some rudimentary Scotty Moore-style guitar and Costello howls a lot (and goes out of tune in several places). Filler, ultimately.

Watch Your Step

Second cousin to 'Secondary Modern'. Nieve's fugue-like organ and a soul beat underpin Costello's dig at the over-inquisitiveness of the Press. A melodica enters dolefully on the bridge while the second verse contains the incongruous allusion 'from Singapore to Widnes'. Clipped and precise to a fault.

New Lace Sleeves

Complex hi-hat and bass drum and a driving Motown bass-line steer this terrific pop/soul vignette. Costello turns in a bravura performance while Nieve drops in some filmic colours to leaven the bitterness of the lyrics. Infidelity, not for the first time, is the subject under rhetorical debate.

From A Whisper To A Scream

A duet with Squeeze's Glenn Tillbrook, nominally in the style of Sam 'n' Dave. A picaresque tale of inebriation and seduction with a crashing treatment from The Attractions, who at various points appear to have turned into The Jam.

Different Finger

Presaging the country excursions of *Almost Blue*, this is an exercise in generic songwriting that Costello admits was 'my attempt to write a Tammy Wynette song'. The punning wordplay endemic in country music is food and drink to the Costello hyper-lexicon – and he doesn't disappoint.

White Knuckles

An ill-judged treatise on domestic violence. Costello seems ambiguous to the action he is depicting ('he didn't mean to hit her but she kept laughing'). The band are seething and magnificent, but it's still a hard song to love. Perhaps Costello had Bonnie Bramlett in mind?

Shot With His Own Gun

Just Nieve at the grandest of grand pianos and Costello's unexpected crooner's warble. This sounds like a Johnny Mercer song with amendments by Sir Andrew Lloyd Webber. Adulterer's guilt is the subject. The extended gun metaphor is clever (as opposed to clever-clever) and Nieve's bewildering ivory-mauling is a constant delight. Nakedly impressive.

Fish 'n' Chip Paper
Workmanlike beat group fare supports another Costello diatribe at the expense of the Fourth Estate. Some uncredited violins appear briefly, then vanish. Costello posits 'winding up in a Hammersmith hotel' as if it were an eternity in Hades. Likeable, nonetheless.

Big Sister's Clothes
All instruments and production by Declan MacManus. Piano strings and kettle drums feature – and his bass playing is nimble to say the least. A song about sexual awakening essayed with a sultry intimacy previously unheard on an Elvis Costello record.

Almost Blue

Label:	F-Beat (UK), Columbia (US)
Released:	October 1981
Chart position:	UK: 7, US: 50
Producer:	Billy Sherrill
Engineer:	Ron 'Snake' Reynolds
Recorded:	July 1981, Columbia Studio A, Nashville

A bold departure or self-indulgent folly depending on your view of country music. This album continues to divide critical opinion. Partly an attempt to put some distance between himself and the swelling ranks of imitators, this collection of country standards curiously finds Costello jettisoning his stylized American twang for a new 'natural' voice.

Why Don't You Love Me Like You Used To Do

The Hank Williams chestnut made over as honky-tonk rockabilly. It's not dissimilar, stylistically, to earlier Costello originals like 'Luxembourg' or, indeed, half the tracks that would make up *King Of America* six years later. Sherrill's odd double-tracking device gives the song a shimmering, out-of-focus quality. Not strictly country.

Sweet Dreams

An aching Don Gibson number and a hit single for Patsy Cline and Loretta Lynn – but not for Elvis Costello. A shame, as it's a beautifully judged vocal, sliding like velvet against John McFee's sinuous pedal steel.

Success

An obscure, cautionary tale of showbiz triumph resulting in domestic dissolution that wouldn't have been lost on Mary Costello. Steve Nieve's piano defines 'plinky-plonky' while Costello sings with the requisite poignant lump in his throat.

I'm Your Toy

Originally titled 'Hot Burrito #2' and possibly the finest song Gram Parsons (along with Chris Etheridge) ever penned. Pleadingly eloquent with a yearning melody that tugs at the heartstrings, it's a perfect vehicle for Costello's effortless range and new-found sensitivity. He really sounds like he means it.

Tonight The Bottle Let Me Down

A witty paean to the limitations of alcohol as the crutch of the broken-hearted, written by Merle Haggard. The Attractions take it at a clip, with John McFee's pedal steel dripping languorous descants over the proceedings with casual abandon. Worldly and spry despite the melancholy undertow of the lyrics.

Brown To Blue
Co-written, unfeasibly, by Johnny Mathis, this is another lovelorn scenario, with the narrator breaking down in the courtroom as his marriage is annulled ('you changed your name from Brown to Jones and mine from Brown to Blue'). Costello just about keeps it on the right side of mawkish.

Good Year For The Roses
Jerry Chesnut's resigned gardening metaphor ('the lawn could stand another mowing, funny I don't even care') is putty in the newly sensitized Costello hands. Trumping even George Jones' excellent 1971 version, Costello (with the Nashville Edition vocal group in celestial harmony) sings with a muted detachment, as if the void left by a departed lover has left him numb rather than sentimental. A triumph of interpretation.

Sittin' And Thinkin'
Charlie Rich's drunk's lament set to The Attractions' jaunty boogie. Costello sounds suitably in his cups, though the song is such a featherweight that even a tanked-up Tom Waits would have trouble lending it gravity.

Colour Of The Blues
Another George Jones vehicle rendered in the classic Nashville honky-tonk style. Costello commands the band with an authoritative performance while Nieve and McFee attempt to wrestle every last nuance from a litany of country clichés. Pleasant enough.

Too Far Gone
Producer Billy Sherrill's own lovesick ballad – once a minor hit for Tammy Wynette. Costello gives it the full treatment from tremulous vibrato wail to declamatory glottal stop. It's a simple but quite lovely song that syrupy strings and airbrushed backing harmonies do their utmost to ruin but, thankfully, don't quite succeed.

Left The Psychotic Bank Clerk
look, c. 1977.

Right With The Attractions
(from left: Pete Thomas,
Bruce Thomas, Elvis
Costello, Steve Nieve).

Left In trademark sneering pose.

Right Obviously not in full artistic control of his early publicity shots, Costello takes singing in the bath to a new level.

Above With Jake Riviera, Costello's ex-manager and subject of a million 'on the road' tales. **Below** Nick Lowe, musician, producer and all-round genius.

Above A rare moment of exuberance.

Below The Brodsky Quartet, partners in one of Costello's more unusual collaborations.

Costello's chameleon-like qualities allow him to perform and collaborate with artists from all parts of the musical spectrum. **Left** Burt Bacharach. **Below** Bob Dylan.

Left Accidents Will Happen. The beard is thankfully now long gone, as sightings of Bigfoot strangely coincided with tour dates.

Below With Cait O'Riordan.

2000: Pleased as punch.

Honey Hush

Bluesman Big Joe Turner (composer of 'Shake, Rattle And Roll') was hardly a country artist, but essaying one of his strident uptempo numbers The Attractions revisit the 1950s sound of Memphis' Sun studios, where a conflation of blues and country helped launch the career of the original Elvis. The latter-day version sings a tad flat on this otherwise likeable filler.

How Much I Lied

Another Gram Parsons tearjerker. This time Costello fails to grasp the nettle and his performance, like that of the band, is muted-verging-on-the-perfunctory. Only Nieve's elegant glissandi seem to have noted the song's pleading tone.

Imperial Bedroom

Label:	F-Beat (UK), Columbia (US)
Released:	July 1982
Chart position:	UK: 6, US: 30
Producer:	Geoff Emerick ('from an original idea by Elvis Costello', according to the sleeve credits)
Engineer:	John Jacobs
Recorded:	February–April 1982, Air Studios, London

With Nick Lowe temporarily banished, Costello and the Attractions get to 'play' in the studio under the guiding hand of one-time Beatles engineer Emerick. Lush, bordering on the baroque, many regard this as Costello's pop masterpiece.

Beyond Belief

A new soft-focus Costello voice introduces this entrancing slice of pop melodrama. Superb shape-shifting drums and exotic, cut-up lyrics ('Just like the canals of Mars and The Great Barrier Reef, I come to you beyond belief') mark out this pulsing, seductive opening gambit.

Tears Before Bedtime

A pendulous, almost jokey backing provides ample opportunity for Costello to trail his terse lyrics about love and betrayal in typically incongruous fashion.

Shabby Doll

Inspired by an old music hall poster, this languidly sung mid-tempo rocker returns Costello to his pun bank ('there's a girl in this dress, there's always a girl in distress') and Bruce Thomas' bass to its wilder flights of fancy.

The Long Honeymoon

Steve Nieve's accordion ushers in a slow, resigned polka ballad. The lyric is pure Raymond Carver, as a wife waits anxiously to see if an errant husband is ever to return. Elliptically autobiographical, then, and strangely catchy despite a meandering tune.

Man Out Of Time

The Attractions recorded two versions of this song about scandal in high places. The finished version recalls Dylan's 'Like A Rolling Stone' in its Hammond-organ-laced grandeur, though it's actually bookended by sections of the thrashy alternative take. Another non-hit as a single but a song of stately majesty that time only burnishes.

Almost Blue

In pure contrast, this is a classic 1940s-style torch ballad that would have fit snugly onto Sinatra's *Only The Lonely* LP. Circumventing pastiche in favour of touching authenticity, Costello proves he's inherited some of his father's vocal nuances. It was later memorably covered by Chet Baker.

... And In Every Home

A wild Nieve arrangement for strings and brass with nods in the direction of The Beatles' 'Penny Lane' wraps itself eccentrically around Costello's bleak tale of redundancy and failing marriages. The setting tends to swamp the lyric.

The Loved Ones

Contrasts the 'glamour' of junkie freefall with the effects on the dependents' family. Not very rock 'n' roll in its adoption of the moral high ground, the impression is doubled by Nieve's inappropriate gameshow organ.

Human Hands

A straightforward love song, thought to be aimed at Bebe Buell, and long a stage favourite. Bruce Thomas turns in a fascinatingly complex bass part which contributes to the positively rococo middle eight – it could almost be Queen. Quite brilliant.

Kid About It

Costello on organ, vibes and hushed vocals. It's an odd song, about 'lying' and 'running away', which returns the narrator once again to Birkenhead. Nostalgic and lovely.

Little Savage

The squalid details of a moribund affair picked over. The band are on top form, pushing the skipping rhythm along unlikely avenues. Costello's surely autobiographical line about 'making love out of something other than spite' indicates a maturing sensibility.

Boy With A Problem

The lyrics are almost completely the work of Squeeze's Chris Difford. The tune, a slow country-ish amble, veers from one cascading melody to another as the narration (about domestic violence, again) unfurls with kitchen-sink realism. There's something unconvincing about Costello's delivery all the same.

Pidgin English

A track recorded in segments then glued together by Geoff Emerick's experienced hand. The Beatles are effortlessly recalled as phased acoustics, mellotrons and a ludicrously loud nylon string guitar come and go like musical traffic. A witty celebration of the power of language.

You Little Fool

The petulance of teenage romance set to a keyboard-laced backing. Psychedelic harpsichords and a Lennon-esque vocal only help this sound like a good 1960s parody. Another non-hit single.

Town Crier

Costello 'does' Curtis Mayfield. The piano intro is essentially the latter's 'People Get Ready'. A beautiful Nieve orchestration recalls Van Dyke Parks' work with Brian Wilson. It inspires Costello's finest vocal performance on the album as he acknowledges his evolution from angry young man to phlegmatic observer ('I'm never gonna cry again, I'm gonna be as strong as them'). Wonderfully plaintive.

Punch The Clock

          Label: F-Beat (UK), Columbia (US)
       Released: July 1983
Chart position: UK: 3, US: 24
      Producers: Clive Langer and Alan Winstanley
      Engineers: Gavin Greenaway and Colin Fairley
       Recorded: January–February 1983, Air Studios, London

> *A creditable stab at state-of-the-art studio pop on first listen, there lurks a bleak world view just below the shiny surface. It re-established Costello as a major chart contender thanks to some successfully extracted singles.*

Let Them All Talk

Pugnacious bass and stentorian drums introduce this brisk slice of blue-eyed soul. The TKO horns reprise the puissant role they played for Dexy's Midnight Runners. An old-fashioned story of lost love, despite the relentlessly upbeat thrust. The proliferation of choruses becomes grating after a while.

Everyday I Write The Book

Aping Smoky Robinson's ability with an extended metaphor, Costello stretches his bibliographical imagery across this jaunty Motown pastiche. Afrodiziak decorate the groove with pleasant harmonies and Costello sings from a far corner of the mix with a relaxed brio.

The Greatest Thing

Hinting subtly at Glenn Miller's 'In The Mood' (a tribute to MacManus *père*?), this is a brass-fuelled, straight-ahead celebration of the power of love, punctuated with cynical caveats (some girls, Costello observes, 'are not to be so easily bribed with a white frock and a ring').

The Element Within Her

Elegantly Beatlesy. A song that, uniquely, treats an electric bar-heater as a metaphor for love. A pure pop construction that hints at Madness on the verses, Lennon on the choruses. The backing vocals are positively choral by the close.

Love Went Mad

Off-the-peg Costello. Nieve is in ivory-tinkling heaven but the rest of the band merely tick over while Costello intones his self-referential query, 'do you have a heart of iron and steel?' Unremarkable, ultimately.

Shipbuilding

It would be hard for anyone to match Robert Wyatt's eye-moistening version of this most sublime of protest songs, but Costello gives it a good try. Dave Bedford's string arrangements are luxuriant and jazz legend Chet Baker lends eloquently mournful trumpet, but Wyatt's absence always looms.

TKO (Boxing Day)

More mighty horns and pumping bass propel this treatise on bullying. The airless production neuters the potentially anthemic chorus and an aimless bridge puts the song out of focus. A shame, as Costello is really giving it everything here.

Charm School

A Bruce Thomas riff flanked by annoying electric piano underpins a tuneless dissection of marriage gone awry. We've been this way before, but never so blandly.

The Invisible Man

Langer and Winstanley call up all their Madness tricks on this bouncy piece of pop jetsam. Costello appears to be singing a different, far more aching song. Nieve persists with the aggravating pins-and-needles piano style he patents on this album.

Mouth Almighty

Listless but revealing. The man with 'the crooner cufflinks and not a hair out of place' is probably Costello, berating the looseness of his own tongue. A better-late-than-never atonement for his 1970s sleight on Ray Charles, perhaps. An underwhelming song, whatever.

King Of Thieves

A story of McCarthy-ite censorship. The Attractions sound like they've been banned from playing anything exciting. The King Of Thieves has obviously snuck in and stolen every last vestige of melody from this drearily worthy monologue.

Pills And Soap

A Grandmaster Flash-inspired anti-Tory diatribe. Costello (aka 'The Imposter') essays a tense vocal and programmes a tinny Linn drum machine while Nieve plays restrained keyboards. The line 'there are ashtrays of emotion for the fag-ends of the aristocracy' once seemed profound and anarchic. A gloomy period piece and the oddest hit single of Costello's career.

The World And His Wife

Once more around the soulful horn merry-go-round. Effulgent and exhilarating music once again masks the bleakest of narratives about marital breakdown and 'the sentimental feeling for the lure of vitriol'. Simultaneously euphoric and depressing.

Goodbye Cruel World

Label: F-Beat (UK), Columbia (US)
Released: June 1984
Chart position: UK: 10, US: 35
Producers: Clive Langer and Alan Winstanley
Engineer: Bob Kraushaar
Recorded: March–April 1984, Sarm West Studio, London

> *'The worst record of the best songs I've written', accord-
> ing to its author – a murky, muted and unlovable
> farrago according to the majority of disappointed fans.
> Costello's nadir to date, however you dress it up.*

The Only Flame In Town

Gary Barnacle's cruise-ship sax sets the tone for this oil-slick of pop-soul insouciance. Daryl Hall sings airbrushed vocal harmonies while The Attractions (as often here) disappear beneath a swathe of Clive Langer's sequencers, synclavers and drum programmes.

Home Truth

A veil of sterile pop clichés obscures one of Costello's most naked-ly autobiographical lyrics about his fatally wounded marriage ('I'd put back the pieces of what's shattered, but I don't know where to start'). Sad, on various levels.

Room With No Number

More confessing. This time the singer's motel tristes with Bebe Buell are laid bare. The tone is resigned, the band restrained to the point of transparency.

Inch By Inch

Originally titled 'Goody Two Shoes' but altered at the last minute to avoid confusion with the Adam Ant song of the same name. Soulful and sophisticated, this carefully constructed vignette about unconsummated love allows the Attractions some breathing space. A relative highlight.

Lovefield

A celebration of al fresco sex that was meant to recall Serge Gainsbourg. Unfortunately it's about as sensual as a fridge. The band are lost again and Costello woefully detached.

I Wanna Be Loved

An old Farnell/Jenkins lovers' rock hit was never going to be more than a thing of pleasant vapidity and it's memorable mainly for Costello's silky vocal. Scritti Politti's Green Gartside provides breathy harmonies and the band some muted pop-reggae flourishes.

The Comedians

A halting 5/4 time signature and a curiously quiet vocal do this clever pop song a disservice. Roy Orbison would later prove there was more to this than the second-rate Madness-style jauntiness that Langer and Winstanley pile on. Supposedly about 'cocaine friendships'.

Joe Porterhouse

A song about family archetypes set at a funeral and to an oddly ruddy tune. The band are more muscular here – Bruce Thomas even gets to execute a few of his meandering bass runs. Still nothing to write home about, it's one of the album's better cuts.

Sour Milk-Cow Blues

A re-write of 'Sleepy' John Estes 'Milk-Cow Blues' – as patented by Elvis Presley at Sun Studios. This is, similarly, cut live in the studio and fairly bristles with rockabilly swagger.

The Great Unknown

A very English song, with Costello ('The unknown soldier') examining the nature of fame by, curiously, setting the narrative at a desultory wedding reception. The music here is insistent but ultimately anodyne.

The Deportees Club

A New York story, like a mini Scorcese drama, set to a crunching rock backing that strains to wrestle itself free from the production strictures. The guitars are like razors. Some vigour at last.

Peace In Our Time

The Imposter's latest protest song gets another airing. Not nearly as affecting as the similar 'Pills And Soap', this errs too heavily toward novelty-song whimsy, despite the line about a 'spaceman in the White House', which became a rallying cry for anti-Reaganites. Costello sings like he means it all the same and, oddly, plays an anvil.

King Of America

Label:	IMPC (UK), Columbia (US)
Released:	May 1986
Chart position:	UK: 11, US: 39
Producers:	J Henry (T-Bone) Burnett and Declan Patrick Aloysius MacManus
Engineer:	Larry Kalman Hirsch
Recorded:	July–August 1985, Sunset Sound, Hollywood

Generally regarded as an artistic renaissance (and the first nail in the coffin for The Attractions – largely absent here), King Of America sees Costello adopting a stellar session cast, rootsy acoustic-based sounds and the Land of the Free as a versatile metaphorical canvas.

Brilliant Mistake

Rising on Mitchell Froom's airy Hammond organ chords, this first paints Reaganite America as a civilization in decline before Costello shifts the onus deftly back onto his own frailties. A mature and stately song, its unforced intimacy sets the tone for the whole album.

Lovable

A throwaway rockabilly workout, co-written with Cait O'Riordan. Los Lobos' David Hidalgo sings a sweet harmony and Costello plays rudimentary rhythm guitar as only he can (he is billed, a tad disingenuously, as 'Little Hands Of Concrete'). Not, actually, that lovable.

Our Little Angel

Ex-Presley side-men James Burton and Jerry Scheff play delicate country-rock guitar and bass respectively in this mysterious tale of after-hours malevolence. The reference to a 'chainsaw running through a dictionary', can't help but invoke Costello's lyrical predilections. Intriguing.

Don't Let Me Be Misunderstood

A minor hit single in the UK, this slightly desperate-sounding version of the Benjamin/Marcus/Calswell standard owes more to The Animals' wracked version than the more skilfully subtle benchmark by Nina Simone (or, indeed, Screamin' Jay Hawkins' addled attempt). Michael Blair from Tom Waits' band plays the catchy marimba part.

Glitter Gulch

More scampering rockabilly dynamics – with James Burton in his wiry element – this is a wry put-down of the entertainment industry, depicted as a flock of vultures circling the public's hapless carcass. It all goes by in a mercurial blur, partly obscuring Costello's razor-sharp lyrics.

Indoor Fireworks

Previously recorded by Nick Lowe, this baleful country tale of marriage grown stale is one of Costello's most aching songs. The lyrics are resigned ('My fuse is burning out') one minute, grandiloquent ('I'll build a bonfire of my dreams, and burn a broken effigy of me and you') the next. The melody, gliding atop doleful twin acoustic guitars, is sublime.

Little Palaces

Just Costello on (unusually dextrous) guitar and mandolin and Jerry Scheff on string bass, this is a Dylan-esque folk song devoted to the plasterboard mundanity of suburban Britain and its attendant undertow of domestic violence. Costello's vocal is raw and aggressive and the spine-tingling instrumental sections like something plucked from the soundtrack to Michael Cimino's *Heaven's Gate*.

I'll Wear It Proudly

Melodramatic, with an exquisite organ theme from Mitchell Froom. Costello is on lacerating lyrical form – never did self-loathing sound so sweet. The lines about being 'a king of fools' and wearing a crown as if it were a dunce's cap echo the sleeve photography. Touchingly honest songwriting.

American Without Tears

A New Orleans-set waltz that pertly recalls 'New Amsterdam'. Joel Sonnier's French accordion lends a gorgeous Cajun piquancy to a true story of English GI brides adrift in the Deep South. Typically, Costello works this into an expanded essay on the cultural allure of the USA. The accordion-led coda is quite lovely.

Eisenhower Blues

A jump-band-style cover of JB Lenoir's obscure 1950s post-war lament. Meat and drink to the veteran band (Tom Canning's piano is pure New

Orleans), this is agreeable and appropriate in tone, but inevitably sounds like the band are enjoying themselves more than we ever will.

Poisoned Rose

The same line-up of jazz eminences (Canning, plus Earl Palmer on drums and Ray Brown on bass) essay a Sinatra-like song about, you guessed it, love gone wrong. Costello sings with admirable control, if a notable lack of emotion, until the dramatic bridge: 'It's just you and me now, coz I threw away the gin'. Classic torch song stuff.

The Big Light

Brisk, Sun Records-style ensemble playing by James Burton, Jerry Scheff and drummer Ron Tutt enliven an odd paean to a hangover which, 'this morning had a personality'. Burton plays a terrific solo, but this, like most hangovers, is soon forgotten.

Jack Of All Parades

Introduced by T-Bone Wolk's regal bass figure and eerie organ by Mitchell Froom, we are practically seduced into this brilliant autobiographical song. Costello is merciless about his past ('I was anybody's boy, but soon the thrill just fades') – seeing redemption in the love of 'one true heart'. Steve Nieve plays an unmistakable cameo on the middle eight. Gorgeous.

Suit Of Lights

The Attractions are reconvened for another of Costello's career self-assessments. He almost seems to choke with passion when delivering some of his most barbed lyrics ('Well it's a dog's life in a rope leash or diamond-stud collar'). The band are restrained, though Nieve's closing Hammond organ is positively hymnal.

Sleep Of The Just

Set in a troop-patrolled Northern Ireland, this is a sombre story of squaddies and rape set to an ironically beautiful, lilting tune. Costello handles a contentious subject with careful sensitivity. As much short fiction as song lyric, if nothing else this signalled yet another significant leap in Costello's maturing lyrical canon. A bleak album-closer, nevertheless.

Blood And Chocolate

Label:	Demon (UK), Columbia (US)
Released:	September 1986
Chart position:	UK: 16, US: 84
Producer:	Nick Lowe
Engineer:	Colin Fairley
Recorded:	May 1986, Olympic Studios, London

Hot on the heels of King Of America *and once again backed solely by The Attractions, Costello saw this as a chance to revisit former glories. With Nick Lowe restored to the producer's podium the band set up as if for a gig and bashed the songs down in one or two takes. That they were falling apart only seems to add to the music's tense, seething velocity.*

Uncomplicated
Raunchy and unbridled. Costello's Telecaster is like razor wire and the band pulsate with a primitive rock urgency. The title is apt – though the lyrics are baffling: 'A horse that knows arithmetic'. Indeed.

I Hope You're Happy Now
Virulent and electric, akin to Bob Dylan and The Butterfield Blues Band's coruscating demolition of the 1965 Newport Folk Festival – the very birth of 'loud 'n' literate' rock music. Costello (billed here

as 'Napoleon Dynamite') sneers for Britain. Revenge never sounded this exciting.

Tokyo Storm Warning

More of the same. A bizarre choice for a single, this being six minutes of churning combo rock and Dylan-esque word torrents. It is as relentless as it is sardonic – Costello quipping about the 'gold paint on the palace gates [which] comes from the teeth of pensioners'. Exhausting.

Home Is Anywhere You Hang Your Head

Softer in attack than the opening salvo, but no less pent-up in its lyric. 'Here comes Mr Misery', is surely autobiographical, though this benign image soon cedes to a more malevolent picture: 'he's contemplating murder again'.

I Want You

The stand-out track. A slow burn of a song with Costello at his most tortured, The Attractions their most threatening. A punctilious contemplation of an ex-lover's new sex life, it's a wholly believable evocation of raw jealousy. Unnerving and quite brilliant, it was a brave single that, unsurprisingly, did not trouble the charts.

Honey Are You Straight Or Are You Blind?

Upbeat, again, and powerfully proportioned in the manner of *This Year's Model*. Costello is in euphoric voice, even if the lyrics dwell dubiously on a doll 'you'd like to pull to pieces'.

Blue Chair

A song left over from the *King Of America* sessions. It sounds like an even older brand of Costello song, though it's allegedly influenced by Prince's 'Manic Monday' – the band certainly attempt a kind of enervated funk 'n' roll. Failed to chart when released as a single.

Battered Old Bird

This is better. Nostalgic and poignant, it's about misbegotten characters from Costello's childhood. Old people are painted as benign figures with the capacity for evil ('next door to them is a man so mild, till he chopped off the head of a visitor's child'). Macabre, then, but with a memorable chorus tune and deft performances all round.

Crimes Of Paris

Gleaming pop with Cait O'Riordan on breathy chorus harmonies. The lyrics are abstruse but the band chime winningly. Costello's voice is sandpaper-harsh by the close.

Poor Napoleon

An intro worthy of Phil Spector, with timpani-like drums and echoing bass. This has a fine vocal melody and an odd line in gender-bending lyrics (Costello, presumably, putting himself into a woman's body as he intones the line about putting his stockings on.) The middle eight contains some nauseatingly seasick organ from the darkest place of Steve Nieve's imagination.

Next Time Round

The Attractions in unfettered form. This is anthemic — the chorus recalls Richie Valens' version of 'La Bamba' — with Costello's voice just about to give out. The next time round for The Attractions would be eight years hence.

Out Of Our Idiot

Label: Demon (UK), Columbia (US)
Released: October 1987
Chart position: UK: did not chart, US: did not chart
Producers: Various
Engineers: Various
Recorded: 1980–87, in various locations

A second round-up of B-sides and rarities.

Seven Day Weekend
A duet between Costello and early reggae star Jimmy Cliff (who also co-wrote the song). A homage to simple hedonism, it's brisk and catchy fare.

Turning The Town Red
The ebullient title track from the Granada TV series *Scully*.

Heathen Town
From the *Punch The Clock* sessions. Too acerbic for that LP, great here.

The People's Limousine
The Coward Brothers' single with T-Bone Burnett. This presaged *King Of America*'s rootsy sound. The tune is good but not brilliant, though the playing is charmingly ragged.

So Young
Not The Corrs song, thankfully. Produced 'at gunpoint' by Nick Lowe at Abbey Road in 1979. A bristling rock-reggae cover from an obscure corner of the Costello record library, it's burdened with a too-dense arrangement.

Little Goody Two Shoes

A out-take from *Imperial Bedroom*. It's a tad perfunctory. Later rewritten as 'Inch By Inch' on *Goodbye Cruel World*.

American Without Tears No2 (Twilight Version)

Lilting, London-recorded alternative to the *King Of America* track. Completely different lyrics and a tinkling xylophone feature.

Get Yourself Another Fool

The 1960s Tucker/Hayward soul ballad given a tender reading by the 1985 Attractions. Nieve's organ solo is mesmerizing.

Walking On Thin Ice

Yoko Ono's best song, with The Attractions subtly economical. Produced by Allen Toussaint in New Orleans during preliminary *Spike* sessions. An unsubstantiated rumour has it that Costello and Ono were briefly 'an item' earlier in the decade. It seems unlikely.

Withered And Died

A gorgeously wrecked Richard Thompson song with Costello on emotional overdrive. Almost a match for the brilliant original.

Blue Chair

Inferior reading of the *Blood And Chocolate* track, from the *King Of America* sessions.

Baby It's You

Burt Bacharach's celebratory love paean delivered as a dolorous duet between Costello and Nick Lowe. Wonderful.

From Head To Toe

A limited edition 1982 single version of a Smokey Robinson obscurity. Originally came free with the *Get Happy!!* album, but only in chart return shops. Accusations of hype and a general furore ensued. The single peaked at No 43.

Shoes Without Heels
The Confederates go through the motions on this countryish *King Of America* leftover.

Baby's Got A Brand New Hairdo
The Attractions with T-Bone Burnett in rockabilly mode. Throwaway.

The Flirting Kind
Another *Blood And Chocolate* reject. Tuneless for all Nieve's extravagant piano flourishes.

Black Sails In The Sunset
Sounds like an *Armed Forces* contender (the melody is more than similar to 'Oliver's Army') but is actually from a year later. The lyrics are impenetrable.

A Town Called Big Nothing (Really Big Nothing)
Part of the soundtrack to Alex Cox's movie *Straight To Hell*. Mariachi guitars, drum machines and Ross MacManus on trumpet try in vain to capture the spirit of Ennio Morricone.

Big Sister
Terrific, fast-paced *Trust* out-take. Should have been included.

Imperial Bedroom
The title track that never was. Jaunty and wry, but not a match for anything on the album of the same name.

The Stamping Ground
Credited to 'The Emotional Toothpaste', another *Imperial Bedroom* sessions casualty. Sounds like a demo.

Spike

Label:	Warners (UK and US)
Released:	February 1989
Chart position:	UK: 5, US: 32
Producers:	Elvis Costello, Kevin Killen and T-Bone Burnett
Engineer:	Kevin Killen
Recorded:	July–August 1988, Ocean Way Studios, Hollywood, Southlake Studios, New Orleans, Windmill Lane Studios, Dublin, Air Studios, London

By Costello's own admission Spike *arose out of frustration with his American record company, Columbia. It ended up on Warners, the final result of four or five entirely different albums he was simultaneously considering. It's certainly an eclectic affair, but a chart success partly on the back of the hit single 'Veronica'. The sleeve is a kitsch abomination.*

This Town

A thrilling intro – processed drums, horror-movie organ and ex-Byrd Roger McGuinn on scintillating 12-string guitar – segues into an assiduous critique of corporate injustice. Cait O'Riordan shakes a maraca and Costello sings the word 'bastard' with unnecessary relish while the extended band (with one Paul McCartney on bass) chime away in plangent fashion.

Let Him Dangle

Another protest song in the style of 'Pills And Soap'. Back in the 1950s teenager Derek Bentley had urged a younger companion, Christopher Craig, to 'let him have it' (referring ambiguously to the gun the latter was carrying) as the two were surprised by a policeman during a petty robbery. Craig proceeded to shoot the constable dead. Bentley was hanged for his outburst (Craig was too young) and the Bentley family had spent forty years protesting his innocence. Latterly Bentley has received a posthumous pardon. Costello's song is passionate and heartfelt and Marc Ribot's jerky guitar scarily conjures up the gibbet.

Deep Dark Truthful Mirror

Featuring New Orleans legend Allen Toussaint on rolling piano and the Dirty Dozen Brass Band on ruminating horns, this could almost be The Band or Doctor John. A surreal tale of self-revelation, the lyrics are plain weird ('a butterfly feeds on a dead monkey's hand') and the tone is dreamlike throughout.

Veronica

Breezy and immediate (doubtless co-writer Paul McCartney's influence) this concerns an elderly relative of Costello's – a lonely spinster looking back on a young lover. McCartney's bass is nimble and Costello's double-tracked vocals apparently fuelled by helium. Melodically it's a superior rewrite of 'Love Went Mad'.

God's Comic

Written on a dreary cruise to the Arctic Circle, Costello reveals this song to be 'about a drunken sleazebag priest dying and arriving in heaven, which is God's MFI warehouse'. Marc Ribot provides plonking Spanish guitar and Mitchell Froom all manner of keyboard textures. God is also pictured as an Andrew Lloyd Webber fan, which seems unlikely.

Chewing Gum

In which a dishevelled pork-pie hat is doffed to Tom Waits. Kirk Joseph plays the funkiest sousaphone and Michael Blair a metal pipe, while an eleven-strong band create a Waitsian vista of surreal clangs, shrieks and belches. Not a total success (Costello just doesn't possess Waits' tarnished but emulsifying larynx), it's a brave effort.

Tramp The Dirt Down

Mystically Celtic, thanks to Donal Lunny's guitar, Davey Spillane's uillean pipes and Steve Wickham's fiddle. This is Costello's elegantly raised finger to ex-British political leaderene, Margaret Thatcher. The idea of gleefully dancing on the grave of a hated nemesis might seem a little arch, even cruel, from this distance. For the many who shared Costello's low opinion of 'The Iron Maiden' this was a rousing clarion call.

Stalin Malone

An instrumental on which Costello doesn't appear, though it once had words which are printed on the inner sleeve. The Dirty Dozen Brass Band do their fulminating jazz thing but it's not terribly memorable for all its freneticism.

Satellite

A prophetic tale of global TV omnipotence that astutely predicts the rise of Rupert Murdoch, Ted Turner and their ilk. Michael Blair plays avant-jazz vibes and The Pretenders' Chrissie Hynde lends aching Ronnie Spector-esque vocals. A prescient, textural song, hamstrung by a negligible melody.

Pads, Paws And Claws

Another McCartney co-write. Costello plays sub-aqua guitar and sings ferally about the 'cat woman' of the title. Eccentric but catchy.

Baby Plays Around

Sad and plaintive. A torch song about jealousy with Costello showing off a new-found dexterity on acoustic guitar. Ingenuous, moving and blessed with the enigmatic line, 'to hold on to that girl I had to let her go'.

Miss Macbeth

Overwrought and overlong. Another song about an old woman —

this time one that local children are convinced is a witch. It turns out they're right. All this unfolds over five minutes of electric bouzoukis, chamberlains and phalanxes of brass that all seem to be playing a different song. Unwieldy, ultimately.

Any King's Shilling

This concerns Costello's paternal grandfather. It's as delicate and economical as its predecessor is overcooked. A seven-piece Irish traditional band (including legendary singer Christy Moore on bodhrán and The Chieftains' Derek Bell on harp) weave a beautifully Celtic backdrop against which Costello sings with touching sincerity about Patrick MacManus' experiences of Dublin after being wounded in the Second World War.

Last Boat Leaving

Costello plays guitar, mandolin, piano, organ and a ship's bell, while Cait O'Riordan contributes something called 'snowbells'. Another misty-eyed story of exile and longing, it proved Costello was just as capable of an evocative landscape when left to his own devices as when surrounded by the cream of session players.

Mighty Like A Rose

Label:	Warner (UK and US)
Released:	May 1991
Chart position:	UK: 5, US: 55
Producers:	Mitchell Froom, Kevin Killen and DPA MacManus
Engineer:	Kevin Killen
Recorded:	Ocean Way Studios, Hollywood, Westside Studios, London

Costello's Beach Boys period. A cast of thousands,

gushing tunes and the bile tap turned off for the most part, it's an album of broad gestures and lyrical grandeur. The last of his albums to really wow the critics.

The Other Side Of Summer
Pays homage to Brian Wilson in its arrangement of bass, piano and vocal quartet. Benmont Tench plays various keyboards (including something called a stereophonic optigon) all of which evoke a palm-fringed paradise. Meanwhile Costello waxes about 'poisonous surf', 'cardboard city' and 'male malice'. Way beyond Beach Boy Brian in its scope – it hardly sold as a single.

Hurry Down Doomsday (The Bugs Are Taking Over)
A twisted 'green' anthem. Costello pictures the world rushing blithely toward Armageddon. Marc Ribot plays 'giant insect mutation and bug attack', or wobbly guitar, if you prefer. Skewed.

How To Be Dumb
A less than gentle riposte to Bruce Thomas' Costello-debunking book *The Big Wheel*, with the seething texture of Dylan's 'Like A Rolling Stone' and as scathing as the latter's 'Positively Fourth Street' in its dismissiveness. Amazingly, the antagonistic duo were soon to work together one last time.

All Grown Up
Redolent of The Beatles' 'She's Leaving Home'. Strings and woodwind by Fiachra Trench (usually to be found on Van Morrison's albums) underscore a resigned ballad of jaded hopes.

Invasion Hit Parade
Ross MacManus is back with his Mariachi trumpet. Oh dear. The song is about a Costello staple – love betrayal, and actually sounds like four songs uncomfortably jammed together. Dense and forgettable.

Harpies' Bizarre

Seduction by class – the title refers to both the high society style magazine *Harper's Bazaar* and the fluffy 1960s American psyche-delic group Harpers Bizarre. Mitchell Froom's harpsichord certainly invokes the latter. It never really gets going.

After The Fall

A dreary acoustic lament in the deep blue style of Leonard Cohen. Marc Ribot's plucked guitar and Steven Soles' harmony vocal per-fectly capture the Cohenite milieu as does the theme of youthful glories atrophied. Another of Costello's brilliant impersonations.

Georgie And Her Rival

A ringing pop song about, appropriately, telephone romance. The Beach Boys seem to hover over the chord changes. The cluttered arrangement spoils it.

So Like Candy

Written with assistance from Paul McCartney, this sounds like an exercise in late 1960s pop classicism. Marc Ribot's sultry guitar is the highlight. The narrative – about a model losing her grip on reality – lacks emotional depth.

Interlude – Couldn't Call It Unexpected No2

Essentially The Dirty Dozen Brass Band in twenty-two seconds of brooding horn crescendo.

Playboy To A Man

A bruising R&B throb in which Costello sounds like a bizarre hybrid of Billy Joel and The Band's Levon Helm. Not very lovely, despite Paul McCartney's co-credit.

Sweet Pear

This could almost be an extract from The Beach Boy's *Pet Sounds*, rising, as it does, on Larry Knetchel's seaside piano and Costello's rarely-heard high falsetto. The Dirty Dozen Brass Band play some aching horn parts and Marc Ribot a sublime guitar solo. The lyrics, essentially a pledge of love, are some of Costello's least affected.

Broken

Written By Cait O'Riordan, and very fine it is. A brooding ambient soundscape supports a folky, dirge-like melody, letting the delicate but direct lyrics quiver in the air. Costello sings with rare restraint: 'But if you leave me then I am broken, and if I am broken then only death remains'. Serious stuff.

Couldn't Call It Unexpected No4

A waltz-time with a hint of New Orleans-via-Dublin in the accordion and banjo arrangement. A celebratory love song given a suitably euphoric accompaniment. Costello's parting lyric, 'I can't believe I'll never believe anything again', is the one, ambiguous note.

The Juliet Letters

Label:	Warners (UK and US)
Released:	January 1993
Chart position:	UK: 8, US: did not chart
Producers:	Kevin Killen, Elvis Costello and The Brodsky Quartet
Engineer:	Kevin Killen
Recorded:	September–October 1992, Church Studios, London

Costello dispenses with rock 'n' roll (and a proportion of his fanbase) for an ascetic diversion into classical music – The Brodsky string quartet providing the only 'backing'. Based thematically around different kinds of epistle, this contains some of Costello's least arch lyrics and,

necessarily, most controlled vocal performances. Two of
the Brodskys are surnamed Thomas, familiarly.

Deliver Us
Forty-nine seconds of gravitas-inducing quartet euphony.

For Other Eyes
Costello's first entry – and he's immediately in fine voice. He inhab-
its the string-scape rather than dominates it. The lyrics return to old
territory – a jealous lover's wounded but vindictive plea. A most
confident opening.

Swine
This time the lyrics reprise an unusually unsentimental gravestone
inscription: 'you're a swine and, that said, it's an insult to the pig'.
Costello's voice is wracked – if a little thespian-sounding. The strings
are an evocative swirl.

Expert Rites
Jacqueline Thomas' elegant cello weaves luminously through this
sadly beautiful melodrama of dead lovers. Costello overuses the
vibrato a tad, but he's impressively unfettered on the soaring chorus. Operatic and impressive.

Dead Letter
A brief, trilling instrumental.

I Almost Had A Weakness
The story of an old woman who leaves her money to an animal
charity. Costello sings the complicated verse with some brio, but the
strings seem to be engaged on more serious business.

Why
Sung from the perspective of an abandoned child, this is achingly

sad, though never mawkish, ('mummy's gone missing, daddy's on fire'). One minute, twenty-six seconds of pure melancholy.

Who Do You Think You Are?

The quartet seem to quote from Vaughan Williams' *A Lark Ascending*, while Costello revisits his old persona. The letter from a jilted lover is full of familiar bile. Believable.

Taking My Life In Your Hands

A complex song. Angular strings give way to a pastoral middle section ornamented with beautiful, tremulous vocals. This time the subject is an unsent love letter full of desperate overtones.

This Offer Is Unrepeatable

Spine-chilling strings lead into a jaunty verse and a lyric constructed from a chain letter's text. It's a bit Rodgers and Hammerstein. The melody wouldn't have been out of place in *Oklahoma*. The lyrics, meanwhile, are scathingly sardonic, ('Just sign on the line, could you possibly write it in blood?').

Dear Sweet Filthy World

Melancholy to a fault. A suicide note is difficult to interpret any other way, frankly. The quartet are wonderfully sonorous here.

The Letter Home

An exile muses on the death of a childhood sweetheart. 'Pump It Up' it ain't. Set in New South Wales between the wars, this practically qualifies as a short story. The nostalgic lyrical passages usher some wonderfully wistful murmuring from the quartet.

Jacksons, Monk And Rowe

Extracted as a single and the nearest thing to old-school Costello on the album. A neat tune and simple, rhythmic string interplay might have benefited from some percussion. It's admirable, nonetheless. The title is a private joke. It's a lot of laughs in the classical world, obviously.

This Sad Burlesque

Composed in honour of yet another general election won by the right-wing Conservative party. Costello sounds wearily resigned – as befits one whose several protest songs on the subject have made no material difference to the outcome.

Romeo's Seance

As romantic as the album gets. The pizzicato strings sound like washboards being scrubbed. Romeo tries to contact the deceased Juliet at the ouija board rather than joining her in death. Whimsical.

I Thought I'd Write To Juliet

Based on a letter Costello received from a female soldier called Constance, embroiled in the Gulf War. The voice is sneering and cynical one minute then soft and meditative as the correspondent admits her sense of fear: 'your words are a comfort, they're the best things I have, apart from family pictures and of course a gas mask'. The quartet impersonate an air raid siren to scary effect.

Last Post

Another short, wordless passage, Michael Thomas' violin eloquently to the fore.

The First To Leave

The strings re-visit Lou Reed's *Street Hassle* as Costello's world-weary tones make the most of a paean to a, no prizes for guessing, dead lover. A convoluted musical backdrop allows Costello the freedom to explore a meandering vocal melody to evocative effect.

Damnation's Cellar

Comi-tragedy. Costello returns to his 'Pills And Soap' voice. The tune is Cole Porter via Robert Wyatt. A sardonic list of those who would be worth saving with the invention of a time machine. The quartet show off their effortless versatility across a shifting musical vista.

The Birds Will Still Be Singing

Poignant lyrics ('spare me the lily-white lilies with the awful perfume of decay') about the inevitability of mortality, given a truly celestial setting by the quartet, obviously in their element. Costello sings like Josef Locke. Wonderful.

Brutal Youth

Label:	Warners (UK and US)
Released:	March 1994
Chart position:	UK: 2, US: 34
Producers:	Mitchell Froom and Elvis Costello
Engineer:	Tchad Blake
Recorded:	October–November 1993, Olympic, Pathway and Church Studios, London

The first Elvis Costello and The Attractions album (de facto, if not in name) since Blood And Chocolate. *Generally perceived as a dignified reunion – if not an earth-shattering one.*

Pony Street

The blurring of the 'generation gap' given a vigorous assault by two thirds of The Attractions and Nick Lowe on bass. Belligerent if not exactly tuneful. It's like they never went away. Almost.

Kinder Murder

The first – and probably only – Costello song to feature the word 'knickers'. A bleak narrative about unwanted pregnancy. The amateurish bass is courtesy of E Costello.

13 Steps Lead Down

This cleverly conflates the Spanish castle where kings were once buried at the foot of thirteen marble steps, with the 'twelve-step' plan to personal fulfilment. Catchy (if not enough to make it more than a minor hit as a single) and caustic, it owes its bubbling undertow to the dextrous presence of Bruce Thomas.

This Is Hell

Costello locates the eternal inferno, naturally enough in a nightclub. More bravura bass runs from Bruce Thomas, otherwise The Attractions are on 'cruise'.

Clown Strike

An odd little song about, well, protesting circus folk. The subtext is dressing up and personal confidence. The band play a gently twisted shuffle. Curious

You Tripped At Every Step

A melody from the same sepia wellspring as Dylan's 'I Threw It All Away', kissed by delicate piano arpeggios from Steve Nieve. A soulful treatise on mental instability. Costello's over-dubbed harmonies invoke The Staple Singers, no less.

Still Too Soon To Know

Bathed in a particularly unflattering echo, Costello 'does' melodramatic country. Confessional but too arch to be as touching as it clearly wants to be. The lyrics are unusually banal, ('will you stay, or will you go …').

20% Amnesia

Angry and pugnacious — this sounds like a patchwork of younger Costello brands and never settles for long enough to establish itself. Nieve's marimba is comically inappropriate.

Sulky Girl

A hit single with a memorable chorus that would have been perfectly at home on *This Year's Model*. Voluptuously played and perfectly, indolently (sulkily?) sung, it's the story of a young girl courting scandal. Terrific.

London's Brilliant Parade

A breezy evocation of Costello's original home town — part nostalgia, part celebration. Borrowing from the mid-1960s sound of The Yardbirds crossed with 'Lola'-period Kinks, a curvaceous melody carries some ambiguous sentiments: 'I'm having the time of my life, or something quite like it'. The place name-checking coda is oddly poignant.

My Science Fiction Twin

An identity crisis set to an abrasive tune. The band are strangely mixed (Froom, as is his wont, bleeds out all the bass tone) and Costello's guitar tries a little too hard to sound 'other-worldly'.

Rocking Horse Road

Detailing a picaresque adventure a sun-stroked Costello undertook in New Zealand, this is an eerie evocation of strangeness in the suburbs. Weird oil-can drums from Pete Thomas and a tune not dissimilar to Smokey Robinson's 'Tears Of A Clown' make this half-formed song curiously memorable.

Just About Glad

Pure Merseybeat, yet reflective and yearning like something off *Trust* essayed by a forty-year-old man, which is almost exactly what it is.

All The Rage

Addressing music critics ('spare me the drone of your advice'), this could contain the album's central statement, ie, 'I'll never be as unhappy as you want me to be'. A searing Richard Thompson-style guitar solo reiterates the point.

Favourite Hour

A gentle ballad – like something from *The Juliet Letters* given a sparse Steve Nieve piano arrangement. Costello addresses life's options – all those 'could have beens'. Essayed with sincerity and dexterity, it even survives some bog-standard 'poetic' imagery, including a reference to a babbling brook.

Kojak Variety

Label:	Warners (UK and US)
Released:	May 1995
Chart position:	UK: 21, US: did not chart
Producers:	Elvis Costello and Kevin Killen
Engineer:	Kevin Killen
Recorded:	April 1990, Blue Wave Studios, Barbados

A fifteen-track trawl through, 'some of my favourite songs, performed with some of my favourite musicians'. The latter, essentially The Confederates with Marc Ribot on guitar and Pete Thomas on drums, are on top form and Costello delights in his interpreter's role. Warners liked it so much they waited five years to put it out.

Strange

An obscure Screamin' Jay Hawkins' B-side given a slick barroom blues treatment redolent of Bob Dylan's mid-1980s albums.

Hidden Charms
A Willie Dixon blues shuffle essayed rather over-reverently.

Remove This Doubt
A Holland-Dozier-Holland rarity Costello learned from a long-deleted Supremes' album. It's deliciously angsty. He overdubs an authentic three-part Motown-style backing 'choir' and Larry Knetchel plays the innards of a piano. Great.

I Threw It All Away
Bob Dylan's sublime tribute to discarded love. The band approximate the sound of the Minnesota bard's *Nashville Skyline*, but Costello sounds bitter rather than the more appropriate phlegmatic.

Leave My Kitten Alone
A no-nonsense take on Little Willie John's jump blues enlivened by James Burton's 'chicken scratch' guitar. Pedestrian session-fodder, otherwise.

I've Been Wrong Before
A laconic satire on the human condition from the pen of jazzer Mose Allison. This owes much to Georgie Fame's clipped 1960s version. Beautifully restrained singing from Costello.

Bama Lama Bama Loo
Attempting a Little Richard song, even an arcane one, is rarely to be advised. No-one will ever match Mr R Penniman's feral screech, though Costello has a go. Strangely lacklustre all the same.

Must You Throw Dirt In My Face
Bill Anderson's broken-hearted country swoon takes us back to *Almost Blue* country. Delicately bruised singing and a twin guitar figure to die for.

Pouring Water On A Drowning Man

A Southern soul toe-tapper once covered by James 'Dark End Of The Street' Carr. Costello is too gruff to reach Carr's transcendent heights.

The Very Thought Of You

Ray Noble's 1930s ballad given a suitably laid-back treatment. Costello croons just like his old man. Lovely.

Payday

Singer-songwriter Jesse Winchester was a major influence on the young Costello. His song here, though possessed of some assiduous lyrics, is a plodding twelve-bar blues dinosaur the band fight a losing battle to spruce up.

Please Stay

Tremulous Lesley guitar by Marc Ribot leads into a touching reading of Bacharach and David's lovelorn weepie. Costello's tuning is a little uncertain, which simply adds to the melodrama.

Running Out Of Fools

Kenny Rogers' atypical torch song rendered, once more, in the Bacharach style. Costello gives it everything while Larry Knetchel's organ and piano make for an unsettling counterpoint.

Days

After all the buried nuggets this seems a too obvious choice. Re-making The Kinks in the style of a Daniel Lanois drone-piece might have seemed like a clever experiment at the time. We know better. Woeful.

All This Useless Beauty

Label:	Warners (UK and US)
Released:	May 1996
Chart position:	UK: 23, US: 53
Producers:	Geoff Emerick and Elvis Costello
Engineers:	Geoff Emerick and John Jacobs
Recorded:	Throughout the second half of 1995,
	Air Studios, London, and various live venues

A collection of songs penned by Costello for other artists – many unrecorded before this. Reassembling The Attractions, The Brodsky Quartet and Geoff Emerick, it was further proof of Costello's peerless craftsmanship in song.

The Other End Of The Telescope
Co-written with Til Tuesday's Aimee Mann, this is a shimmering ballad with a theme of Catholic guilt and a sinuous tune. Seductive.

Little Atoms
A murmuring sequencer and gorgeous flashes of piano from Steve Nieve underscore this lyrically dense, vaguely biblical song. Despite a reasonable melody, it's ultimately unfathomable. No wonder nobody wanted to cover it.

All This Useless Beauty
Recorded by folk singer June Tabor on her *Angel Tiger* album (and not as good as the song 'Against The Stream' Costello also wrote for her). A serene ballad with a stately chord progression, wistful chorus and dolorous bassoon.

Complicated Shadows

Written for Johnny Cash but sounding more like Bob Dylan in his religious phase. A graveyard setting, loping drums and Costello sneering about the inevitable hand of fate. The pure punk coda is edited from a 1995 New York concert.

Why Can't A Man Stand Alone

Piano and organ, in the Southern soul style, propel this Bobby Bland-aping ballad. Composed for soul star Sam Moore though he never recorded it (his wife allegedly noted racist undertones in the lyrics, though it's impossible to see why). A neat treatise on gender roleplay.

Distorted Angel

Complex and downbeat, this verges on the sophistication of Steely Dan in its electric piano-soaked arrangement. Costello unfurls some brilliantly keening falsetto notes on the coda.

Shallow Grave

Co-composed with Paul McCartney, this is skewed rockabilly with Costello essaying an impression of Marc Ribot's eccentric guitar style. The shovelled-on wackiness can't disguise the song's pedestrian nature. Mercifully brief.

Poor Fractured Atlas

Steve Nieve cannibalizes Beethoven's 'Moonlight Sonata' on the piano and Costello sings wryly about masculine insecurity ('waving his withering pencil as if it were a pirate's cutlass'). The 'men's movement' stops here.

Starting To Come To Me

Inspired, allegedly, by re-runs of Mary Tyler Moore comedy shows, this is an ungainly rocker, with Nieve at his most insouciant on kitsch Hammond organ. Forgettable flotsam, really.

You Bowed Down

Written for Roger McGuinn of The Byrds and, thus an exercise in chiming twelve-string plangency. A brilliant pastiche, the lyrics may refer to fractious dealings with Warner Brothers. McGuinn's own version sounds less like The Byrds than this.

It's Time

This was aimed at blues singer Bonnie Raitt – and it's easy to imagine her cracked, soulful voice wrapping around this tale of squandered love. Costello gets close to hysterical in places here, while Nieve reprises several of his most symphonic moments. Oddly epic.

I Want To Vanish

Written for an aborted second LP with The Brodsky Quartet. Nieve arranges their strings (plus woodwind) around his parlour piano and Costello yearns warmly for sweet exile. ('I'm certain as a lost dog pondering a signpost'). Quite lovely.

Painted From Memory

Label:	Warners (UK and US)
Released:	October 1998
Chart position:	UK: 32, US: 42
Producers:	Burt Bacharach and Elvis Costello
Engineer:	Kevin Killen
Recorded:	April 1998, Ocean Way Studios, Los Angeles, Right Track Studios, New York

An unlikely collaboration on the surface – the king of angst meets the eminence grise *of lounge – this was essentially a partnership of pop classicists (and Costello had been covering Bacharach songs as far back as the*

*first Stiff tour in 1977). Cynical critics saw it as evidence
of Costello 'selling out'. It works best when Costello eases
up on the sometimes stylized lyrics, but it's impressive
even when he doesn't.*

The Darkest Place

The Bacharach hallmark is immediately recognizable as this comes
gliding in on muted piano chords before unfolding like a second
cousin to 'Do You Know The Way To San Jose?'. Costello's lyric is
resigned ('you may laugh but pretty girls look right through me') but
there is redemption in the tone of his voice.

Toledo

A nagging tune and signature trumpet underpin a typically Costelloian epistle that dwells on the details of an adulterous dalliance. Spoilt
by the unnecessarily syrupy backing singers.

I Still Have That Other Girl

Concise and aching. This time adultery is nipped in the bud. The
twenty-four-piece orchestra swoon magnificently. Dionne Warwick
(Bacharach's original muse) would soar on this gorgeous updraught
of a melody. Exquisitely wracked, symphonic pop music.

This House Is Empty Now

An effortlessly lovely backing, all accordion and glockenspiels, leads
into a sad ballad redolent of 'Good Year For The Roses' in its post-
affair desolation. Costello overdoes the vocal vibrato – and the lyrics
are ersatz MOR fare. The guitar solo is horrible, too.

Tears At The Birthday Party

Using a childrens' celebration as a flimsy metaphor for jealousy
('now I see you share your cake with him'), this is unremarkable.
Bacharach could have arranged this in his sleep. Perhaps he did.

Such Unlikely Lovers

A taut electric piano riff ushers in an optimistic song about chance meetings and unexpected love. There's too much backing vocal saccharine to allow the narrative to flow properly.

My Thief

An old-fashioned ballad – closer to Hoagy Carmichael than Burt Bacharach. Sophisticated orchestrations and evocatively intoned words about unobtainable love feature. They don't write them like this any more – except chez Bacharach and Costello. Beautiful.

The Long Division

Loquacious electric pianos and a soulful groove nimbly change the mood. The liquid backing is pure economy. Costello's mathematics puns border on the tedious – a great vocal, despite this.

Painted From Memory

Sinatra-like in its blue wistfulness, this nostalgic heartbreaker is sung to the accompaniment of regal piano and acoustic guitar with eddying strings for punctuation. The lonesome melody is close to that of Kurt Weill's 'Lost In The Stars'.

The Sweetest Punch

Steve Nieve features on a variety of keyboards. Suitably, this is as near as the album gets to a more familiar Costello sound. It's the first to highlight serious rock drums while Bacharach's piano and strings noodle at the margins. An obvious pugilistic metaphor gets milked. Superfluous, ultimately.

What's Her Name Today?

Returning to the relaxed ambience of Bacharach's 1960s work, Costello contrasts the luscious melody with a dark tale of rejected lovers. He sings the pay-off line with spine-chilling passion.

God Give Me Strength

Written for the feature film *Grace Of My Heart* and appropriately widescreen in its ambition. A tour-de-force vocal from Costello – bruised on the verses, celestial on the falsetto choruses – with lyrics that recall erstwhile Bacharach co-writer Hal David. ('She was the light that I bless, she took my last chance of happiness'.) Sung with thorough believability. Terrific.

OTHER COSTELLO ALBUMS

Live At The El Mocambo

Label: Columbia (Canada only)
Released: June 1978

Canada-only promo – limited to 500 copies, subsequently much-bootlegged.

Almost New

Released: November 1982
Australia-only mini-album compilation.

The Best Of Elvis Costello – The Man

Released: April 1985
The first of the man's many compilation LPs, issued on IMP. Number 8 in the UK.

The Courier

Released: July 1988
The soundtrack to a Dublin-set film featuring Cait O'Riordan. Costello contributes six instrumentals.

Girls, Girls, Girls

Released: October and November 1989
(in two volumes)
Another career overview – this time on Demon. Reached Number 67 in the UK.

GBH – Soundtrack

Released: July 1991
Co-composed with Richard Harvey, this was the music to playwright Alan Bleasdale's Channel 4 TV series.

Now Ain't The Time For Your Tears

Released: May 1993
Wendy James' entirely Costello-penned, tailor-made album. It proved to be her career's valedictory gesture – though a single, 'London's Brilliant' (co-written by Costello and Cait O'Riordan), was a minor UK hit.

The Very Best Of Elvis Costello And The Attractions

Released: October 1994
More 'greatest hits' designed to line the coffers of Demon Records. Unfortunately it only staggered as far as Number 57.

Deep Dead Blue

Released: August 1995
A live mini-album documenting a one-off concert with American avant-garde guitarist Bill Frisell at London's South Bank arts complex. Released on the classical Nonesuch label. Didn't trouble any charts.

Jake's Progress – Soundtrack

Released: October 1995
Another TV soundtrack collaboration with Richard Harvey and Alan Bleasdale.

For The First Time In America

Released: December 1996
Subtitled, 'Elvis Costello and Steve Nieve Live and Acoustic. Five nights. Five Cities'. Originally a promo-only item, it received an extremely limited edition released by Warners in the US only.

Extreme Honey:
The Very Best Of The Warner Bros Years

Released: October 1997
Perhaps the best way to consume Costello's 'difficult' album period. Contains the otherwise unavailable Eno collaboration 'My Dark Life'. Number 37 in the UK. The US promotional budget for this record is alleged to have been a paltry $1,000, hence no show there.

Songs Of Elvis Costello – Bespoke Songs, Lost Dogs, Detours And Rendezvous

Released: May 1998

A comprehensive corralling of the best cover versions of Costello originals from the likes of Robert Wyatt, Norma Waterson, Christy Moore, Roy Orbison and Chet Baker. Illuminating sleevenotes by the man himself. Charted nowhere.

The Very Best Of Elvis Costello

Released: August 1999

The latest round-up of Costello hits – including 'She', his 1999 contribution to the hit movie Notting Hill. Reached Number 4 in the UK, 29 in the US a a result.

Mad About The Wrong Boy (The Attractions)

Released: September 1980

Like Graham Parker's Rumour, Costello's gifted backing band thought they possessed the requisite arsenal to strike out on their own. The sad truth remains that, like so many original, versatile masters of their instruments, The Attractions make lousy singers and – the occasional tricksy Steve Nieve melody apart – plodding songwriters. The best efforts here – 'Arms Race', 'Taste Of Poison' – are the ones that sound like the Governor might have written them (before screwing up the paper and starting again). Dull power pop, ultimately.

SINGLES

These are the official, non-promo, UK singles – detailing format oddities only where relevant. US and European releases are similar, though B-sides and formats vary in such profusion that space doesn't allow their full inclusion. Major US singles unreleased in the UK are listed.

Less Than Zero/Radio Sweetheart – March 1977

Alison/Welcome To The Working Week – May 1977

(The Angels Wanna Wear My) Red Shoes/Mystery Dance – July 1977

Watching The Detectives/Blame It On Cain (live)/Mystery Dance (live) – October 1977

(I Don't Want To Go To) Chelsea/You Belong To Me – March 1978

Pump It Up/Big Tears – June 1978

Radio Radio/Tiny Steps – October 1978

Oliver's Army/My Funny Valentine – February 1979

Accidents Will Happen/Talking In The Dark/Wednesday Week – May 1979

I Can't Stand Up For Falling Down/Girls Talk – January 1980

High Fidelity/Getting Mighty Crowded – April 1980

New Amsterdam/Dr Luther's Assistant/Ghost Train/Just A Memory – June 1980

Clubland/Clean Money/Hoover Factory – December 1980

Watch Your Step/Luxembourg (US only) – February 1981

From A Whisper To A Scream/Luxembourg – February 1981

Good Year For The Roses/Your Angel Steps Out Of Heaven – September 1981

Sweet Dreams/Psycho (live) – December 1981

I'm Your Toy (live)/Cry, Cry, Cry/Wondering – April 1982

I'm Your Toy (live)/My Shoes Keep Walking Back To You/Blues Keep Calling/Honky Tonk Girl (12") – April 1982

You Little Fool/Big Sister/The Stamping Ground – June 1982

Man Out Of Time/Town Cryer (alternate version) – July 1982

Man Out Of Time/Town Cryer/Imperial Bedroom (12") – July 1982

From Head To Toe/The World Of Broken Hearts – September 1982

Party Party/Imperial Bedroom – November 1982

(The Imposter) Pills And Soap/Pills And Soap (extended version) – May 1983

Everyday I Write The Book/Heathen Town – June 1993

Everyday I Write The Book/Heathen Town/Night Time – June 1983

Let Them All Talk/The Flirting Kind – September 1983

(The Imposter) Peace In Our Time/Withered And Died – April 1984

I Wanna Be Loved/Turning The Town Red – June 1984

I Wanna Be Loved/Turning The Town Red/I Wanna Be Loved (extended version) – June 1984

The Only Flame In Town/The Comedians – August 1984

The Only Flame In Town ('Version Discotheque')/Pump It Up (1984 dance mix)/The Comedians – August 1984

Green Shirt/Beyond Belief – April 1985

Green Shirt/Beyond Belief/Green Shirt (extended mix)(12") – April 1985

(The Coward Brothers) The Peoples' Limousine/They'll Never Take Her Love From Me – June 1985

Don't Let Me Be Misunderstood/Baby's Got A Brand New Hairdo – January 1986

Don't Let Me Be Misunderstood/Baby's Got A Brand New Hairdo/Get Yourself Another Fool – January 1986

Tokyo Storm Warning (Parts One And Two) – August 1986

Tokyo Storm Warning/Black Sails In The Sunset (12") – August 1986

I Want You (Parts One And Two) – October 1986

I Want You/I Hope You're Happy Now (12") – October 1986

Blue Chair/American Without Tears No2 (Twilight Version) –
    January 1987

Blue Chair/Shoes Without Heels/American Without
    Tears/American Without Tears No2 (Twilight Version)

A Town Called Big Nothing/Return To Big Nothing – May 1987

A Town Called Big Nothing/Return To Big Nothing/A Town Called
    Big Nothing (The Long March) (12") – May 1987

Veronica/You're No Good – January 1989

Veronica/You're No Good/The Room Nobody Loves In/Coal Train
    Robberies (12") – January 1989

Baby Plays Around/Poisoned Rose/Almost Blue/My Funny Valentine
    – May 1989

Baby Plays Around/Point Of No Return Almost Blue/My Funny
    Valentine (10" and 12" versions) – May 1989

The Other Side Of Summer/Couldn't Call It Unexpected No4
    – April 1991

The Other Side Of Summer/Couldn't Call It Unexpected
    No4/The Ugly Things (12" and CD) – April 1991

So Like Candy/Veronica (demo)/Couldn't Call It Unexpected
    No4/Hurry Down Doomsday (The Bugs Are Taking Over)(12"
    and CD) – September 1991

Jacksons, Monk And Rowe/This Sad Burlesque (cassette) –
    February 1993

Jacksons, Monk And Rowe/Interview (CD) – February 1993

Sulky Girl/A Drunken Man's Praise Of Sobriety – February 1994

Sulky Girl/Idiophone/A Drunken Man's Praise Of Sobriety/Sulky
    Girl (album version)(CD) – February 1994

Thirteen Steps Lead Down/Do You Know What I'm Saying? – April
    1994

Thirteen Steps Lead Down/Puppet Girl/Basement Kiss/We
    Despise You (CD) – April 1994

You Tripped At Every Step/You've Got To Hide At Every Step –

July 1994

You Tripped At Every Step/Step Inside Love/You've Got To Hide Your Love Away/Sticks And Stones (CD) – July 1994

London's Brilliant Parade/London's Brilliant (cassette) – November 1994

London's Brilliant Parade/My Resistance Is Low/Congratulations/ London's Brilliant/Head To Toe (12" and CD)

Its Time/Life Shrinks/Brilliant Disguise (CD) – May 1996

Little Atoms/Almost Ideal Eyes/Just About Glad/Why Can't A Man Stand Alone? (One of four CD singles released this month) – July 1996

The Other End Of The Telescope/Almost Ideal Eyes/Basement Kiss/Complicated Shadows (cashbox version) – July 1996

Distorted Angel/Almost Ideal Eyes/All This Useless Beauty (performed by Lush)/Little Atoms (DJ Food mix)/Little Atoms (polished glass mix) – July 1996

All This Useless Beauty/Almost Ideal Eyes/The Other End Of The Telescope (performed by Sleeper)/Distorted Angel (Tricky remix) – July 1996

Toledo/Tears At The Birthday Party (live)/Inch By Inch/Fever (live) – April 1999 (CD)

Toledo/Such Unlikely Lovers (live)/Baby Plays Around (live) – April 1999(CD)

She/This House Is Empty Now/The Sweetest Punch – July 1999

She/Painted From Memory/The Sweetest Punch – July 1999

THREE

THE LEGACY

At forty-six, Declan MacManus has reached the phase of life where it is natural to sit back and take stock, to make a mental inventory of what has been accrued and of that which has still to be achieved. After due consideration it is hard to imagine him not being as pleased as punch (the odd regretful moment aside) with the former, while an apparently boundless appetite for novel musical ventures surely finds him contemplating a future studded with enticing possibilities, odd collaborations and untried disciplines. It is a sanguine state of affairs shared by few of his peers.

What the mature Elvis Costello has become is that rarest of things in the tendentious, ego-driven industry in which he has plied his trade these last twenty-five years or so: a healthy, wealthy, wise and well-balanced individual. He maintains a laudably sceptical attitude toward his own 'myth' and a forward-looking mentality that generally (if not exclusively) eschews easy commercial options in favour of bold artistic challenges. Again, there are few artists of his vintage about whom the same can be said.

Of course for a pop classicist like Costello 'artistic challenge' is a relative term – he's yet to turn in a pulsating new take on free-form jazz or a novel, noodling, post-rock album, for example – though nothing should be discounted. Certainly, for a one-time raging, guitar-mauling iconoclast to sculpt a suite of de-luxe, bitter-sweet lounge songs with Burt Bacharach, or dabble in odd classical polyphony with The Brodsky Quartet, provides evidence of a terrifically unpredictable career curve.

Costello has never been afraid of pushing the stylistic envelope of pop, even if his sense of experimentation is firmly rooted in the timeless possibilities of song. Indeed, while Costello's is a broad church, it is exclusively one founded on the implacable templates of twentieth century popular music – rock 'n' roll, R&B, country, folk, jazz-balladeering, theatrical song and so on. So while his protean calling is admirable and rare, the parameters within which his muse is played out increasingly date him. However much he attempts to stab forward, he is always restrained by the tendrils of pop classicism with which his enthusiasms have so long been entwined. One Tricky remix and the drum machine dalliance of 'Pills And Soap' aside, Costello has never had much truck with the nominally dance-music-derived underground which is really the last remaining engine of stylistic change in contemporary popular music. Ultimately, perhaps, Costello has more in common with his father's generation than with his son's.

That said, Costello – like few of the contemporaries that emerged from the liberating Year Zero of punk – retains a phenomenally questing spirit and a sense of integrity, purity even, that he clings to, often at the expense of album sales, whilst engendering a bewildering spectrum of critical receptions. The increasing 'selectivity' of his audience seems not to bother him a jot, as he explained in a recent interview with *The Guardian's* Mark Cooper: 'The measure of failure has become much more drastic, but I also know there are singers and bands who would be delighted by my smallest success. I am very proud to have had such a curious audience.'

Even if his more recent pursuits do occasionally reek of self-indulgence ('self-obsessed and charmless', is how critic and one-time EC disciple Stuart Maconie described the bearded Costello of the early 1990s, echoing the most common latter-day snipe), he can never be accused of not hurling himself into untried territories, often (and this is telling for such an obviously musically literate and knowing individual) with an ingenue's happy abandon. Most of the time, these days, he seems to be genuinely enjoying himself – just look at the inner sleeve photos of *Painted From Memory*, with Costello and Bacharach mugging for the camera – the former's boyish grin betraying a genuine sense of gleeful disbelief at the company he's now keeping. Far from 'charmless', on the face of it.

The same kind of wide-eyed but amused self-deprecation oozes from the extensive and insightful sleeve notes he's recently penned for the CD reissues of his weighty album back catalogue. It's all a far cry from the spitefully raging catharsis of that 1977 incarnation.

True, he may have released too many albums in the 1990s (eleven, including compilations and soundtracks) to allow any individual outing the weight of significance that an absence from the fray would inevitably have invited, but within that eclectic glut nestles some of his most incisive writing and luminous singing. If one plays some of his more poignant and thoughtful compositions of recent times, such as 'Deep Dark Truthful Mirror', 'The Other Side Of Summer' or 'The Birds Will Still Be Singing', for example, alongside earlier, equally serious-themed works of the calibre of 'Alison', 'Beyond Belief' or 'Indoor Fireworks', to take another arbitrary sample, the later period's songs' refined sophistication and, crucially, life-affirming humanity glows like a winter hearth fire by comparison. But his has not been simply a considered ascent (descent?) into the mellowness of middle age. Far from it. There's nothing mild-mannered about his 1990s albums, it's just that now anger, bitterness, sadness and wonder are more skilfully – often achingly – expressed. For whatever the fierce brilliance of Costello's most celebrated 1970s and '80s oeuvre, it is resolutely the work of a man struggling to come to terms with his own inadequacies; redemptive at best, pained at worst. Almost a quarter of a century on, he seems to have achieved some kind of equilibrium. Not so much resigned to the world but, rather, philosophical about its privations and grateful for its gifts.

So, mature in thought and deed, apparently happily married to Cait O'Riordan, and finally berthed at a record company and management set-up (essentially, he manages himself) that affords maximum freedom to follow his meandering muse, Costello is no longer a 'Man Out Of Time', or a 'Boy With A Problem', but a respected, if still spiky, pillar of British musical life. These days he's 'Uncomplicated' and 'Just About Glad'. And whatever the man is gearing up for next he can rest assured that his energetic odyssey along the motorways and B-roads (not to mention the odd dirt track) of pop has left a plume of influence that continues to hover subtly over the musical landscape.

Elvis Costello's impact on the volatile late 1970s pop universe is difficult to imagine from so great a distance – but it was hugely important for the longevity of the era's rock dinosaur-banishing *zeitgeist* that an artist would emerge from within its ranks capable of transcending the transient, knee-jerk thrills of buzz-saw punk and its increasingly ersatz nihilist gesturing. Someone, as it were, who could carry the fight into the mainstream.

Already a 'veteran' of the pub rock demi-monde, Costello

(with valuable input from the wily Jake Riviera) was punctilious and prescient in the manner with which he welded punk's scorching aggression to the measured musicality of the 'greats' of rock, pop and jazz he'd absorbed initially from his parents' record collections and later from his own studious investigations into pop and rock genealogy. For Costello, punk rock was the essential catalyst that allowed a prodigious talent (and a lot of pent-up anxiety) a focus, a stage and an audience. It also provided a crutch by which his more timeless concerns – the artfully-structured song form, the power and mutability of language – could tiptoe into the spotlight.

Unlike fellow 'parasites' hitching a ride on punk's bandwagon – notably The Police, for whom chart success was always a transparent *raison d'etre* – Costello's youthful anger was real, and he was soon carrying his sense of dysfunctional frustration into songs that outwardly bore few of punk's stylistic hallmarks. As the American critic Greil Marcus notes in his collection of writing on punk, *In The Fascist Bathroom* (itself a title worthy of the young Costello): 'Far too weird in looks and stance to have had a chance before the Sex Pistols trashed all pop rules in London, Costello drew on punk's spirit but escaped its labels.' Marcus goes on to identify the more significant wellsprings of exasperation and self-doubt that were Costello's true creative engines: 'When he said he was driven by revenge and guilt, he made those emotions poles of a whole world... He was an original: bitter, cruel, and funny, as much his own target as anyone else was.'

Costello's other great asset was his ability, again honed at the workbench of pop classicism, to fashion an effulgently memorable tune – and it was this facet of his early work which brought both success in the radio-tyrannized USA and, soon after, a steady stream of imitators. Being volubly enraged to an anthemic chorus (typified by 'Radio Radio' or 'Pump It Up') made for a far more appealing blueprint to many than the similar but far more scarifying storm and stress (not to mention explicit anarchism) of the Sex Pistols. Besides, the early Attractions were always more souped-up 1960s garage rock (with Steve Nieve's organ a dead ringer for that of garage cult combo, ? And The Mysterions) than blitzkrieg punk, and to American audiences this was music redolent of the 'British Invasion' of the mid-1960s, only with a dash of 1970s amphetamine and lashings of lyrical acid for added spice. Punk-aware kids and their 'golden era'-steeped parents alike could marvel at the Costello phenomenon. He was simultaneously a hip-loser firebrand for the angst-ridden adolescent and a hip neo-Dylan for its credit card-generation parents.

Costello's initial chart success – particularly in the US – was instrumental in altering music business perceptions about punk (in fact, it helped suggest a means by which the major record companies could invest in a genre that had initially sought, somewhat fancifully, to bring the industry to its knees) and ushered in a flotilla of artists engaged more with the possibilities of energetic guitar pop than with the rancorous agendas and political proselyting of punk.

In the States, Costello contemporaries Blondie were cutting a similar swathe through old-school preconceptions, achieving similar recognition for their fusion of CBGB's punk cool, singer Deborah Harry's svelte indolence and a clutch of knowing pop songs soaked in Spector-esque tunefulness. It was from such acorns that the catch-all phenomenon of new wave music grew. Essentially anything upbeat and sprightly played by people in tight jeans and skinny ties (an emblematic sartorial choice of which both Costello and the Blondie boys were equally keen) new wave, like punk (though the labels were often, as they continue to be, conflated) eschewed long guitar solos and portentous theatrics in favour of a tinny anthemicism. In tandem with the likes of Blondie, then, Costello inadvertently helped launch the (generally long-lived) careers of new wave bands like The Knack, The Feelies and The GoGos in the US, The Pretenders, Squeeze and Joe Jackson in the UK. Other, already extant, outfits like Huey Lewis And The News (once Costello's backing band, Clover) and The J Geils Band found a new focus for their 1960s-derived musical energies as they began successfully remoulding themselves partly in Costello and The Attractions' image.

Costello's influence on British bands was even more direct and profound. Successful singer-songwriter Joe Jackson's entire act was as a Costello *manqué* – even down to the frustrated sexual countenance of songs like 'Is She Really Going Out With Him?' South Londoners Squeeze, meanwhile, picked up on Costello's lyrical sententiousness – typically in songs like 'Up The Junction' and 'Pulling Mussels (From A Shell)'. There were many more. The Jags would have made an excellent Attractions covers band, while Clive Gregson (who like Costello would later gravitate successfully towards folk forms alongside singer Christine Collister) seemed to ape Costello's every move, only with lamentably banal songs and a nerdish image only a mother could love, which made Costello look like Robert De Niro by comparison. It's probably better not to dwell on the mercifully brief 'careers' of Elton Motello, Clive Culberstone or Moon Martin.

Unsurprisingly, new wave music would always be a betrayal to some – anodyne, combed-hair punk – a phenomenon whose, in reality tenuous, connection to Costello's work would take harsher critics years to forgive or forget. With hindsight this pillorying (Blondie received similar vilification from New York's hardline punk critics) seems terribly unfair on Costello. After all, he and The Attractions had mixed it with the best of 1977's angry brigade, often fighting on the very front line of punk itself. Remembering touring with the band during those visceral times, Suicide singer Alan Vega – himself no stranger to the phlegm and fists of an angry, speeding punk mob – recalls: 'There was a riot every night with Elvis. Some nights they wouldn't go on. They were crazed. When we hooked up it was the ninth, tenth month of their tour and I think they'd been doing a lot of speed... one night we had this big thing in Belgium... they never got on! It was a police riot – they came in with tear gas!'.

That Costello had earned his stripes in these punk skirmishes was not lost on everyone, however. For many the fact that he was able to survive punk's initial onslaught and then go on to forge a career whose range and versatility maintained an implicit questioning ethos, if not always a manifest one, made his maturing output all the more relevant. Costello was the kind of artist fans could grow up with, regarding each of his stylistic leaps in the dark as benchmarks in their own lives. His was not always a perfect paradigm of personal 'growth', but he generally presented the best visible example of how to survive punk and stay relevant.

With that in mind it is possible to see how Costello's influence on British songwriting of the 1980s and '90s, while being less obvious than in his vitriol-dressed salad days, is perhaps more keenly felt. By maintaining a dedication to a broadly left-wing political agenda in a litany of protest songs from 'Less Than Zero' to 'Let Him Dangle' via 'Pills And Soap' and 'Shipbuilding' (songs that run the stylistic gamut from febrile rock to torch-jazz and quasi-rap), Costello proved that an idealogue need not post his colours to obvious anthems or rallying points (though his involvement with Live Aid and the Free Nelson Mandela campaign proved he wasn't above collective action).

Costello maintains an ability to wrestle sublime observational insights from the most mundane or obvious narratives –

think of the emotional pull that a song like 'Shipbuilding' exerts by the understated evocativeness with which a family's everyday concerns are used to express the horror of war. And he doesn't reserve this for songs of a specifically political hue. As Greil Marcus observes of *King Of America*: 'The singer cries out against some great wrong, but while he makes the song[s] impossible not to understand emotionally, the exact nature of the great wrong evades him, forcing him into poetry.'

Thus, his influence has seeped out into the work of a host of British songwriters with social concerns high on their agenda, but who have the intelligence to locate their concerns within a wider emotional landscape. It would be difficult to imagine Billy Bragg's pun-soaked dissections of British social mores (in particular songs such as 'New England', 'The Milkman Of Human Kindness' or 'Greetings To The New Brunette') without Costello's imprimatur. Indeed Bragg has often performed Costello songs – his late-1980s live readings of 'Little Palaces', for instance, being memorably impassioned. That Bragg has also exhibited a fondness for a sort of journalistic pop classicism ('Levi Stubbs' Tears', for example) also bears comparison with the Costello role model.

The Beautiful South's Paul Heaton is another significant contemporary songwriter for whom Costello's melding of winsome melody, barely withheld spite and wry, demotic observation is surely the prototype. A simple head-to-head between Heaton's 'Let Love Speak Up Itself' with most of *Imperial Bedroom*, his 'Pretenders To The Throne' with much of Costello's *King Of America* or, indeed, Heaton's 'Rotterdam' with Costello's 'New Amsterdam', points up similarities of style (if anything Heaton ranges over even larger tracts of pop's panoply than Costello – he's certainly more fearless when it comes to deconstructing MOR modes), satire and lyrical astuteness.

But it's not just Costello's politicized attitude or neo-punk troubadour's persona that have found favour with contemporary musicians. Bristol's wild man of skewed trip hop, Tricky, has sampled 'Pills And Soap' (and, as mentioned, has been rewarded with a rare remix for Costello's 'Distorted Angel'). Another high profile fan is Radiohead's Thom Yorke, who describes Costello thus: 'he can be very emotional without being personal, that's his gift'. Certainly, some of Costello's self-lacerating angst can be found in Yorke's own songs – particularly 'Creep' or 'No Surprises' – though it's hard to agree with Yorke about Costello's lack of personal revelation in song. A casual listen to 'I Want You' or 'I'll Wear It Proudly' would certainly seem to argue otherwise. Ask Bebe Buell.

Elsewhere Costello's fusion of timeless pop melody, barbed narration and acute observation can be traced in 'traditionalist' songwriters of the current era like Americans Elliott Smith and Freedy Johnston or Canadian Ron Sexsmith, while the late, much-fêted Jeff Buckley, perhaps the closest thing in recent times to the transcendent 1960s troubadours (including Jeff's dad, Tim Buckley) who inspired Costello, predictably pronounced himself a fan (Costello repaid the compliment by giving Buckley a slot during his 1995 curatorship of London's Meltdown Festival).

That such a diverse raft of artists have chosen to essay Costello's songs (who else could assemble an album of cover versions by artists including George Jones, Was Not Was, Paul McCartney, The Dubliners, Roy Orbison and June Tabor?) is testament to the versatility and consistent quality of the man's writing; punk rock be damned.

There's really no one to match him in terms of sustained, quality English songcraft – the nearest thing is probably Fairport Convention founder Richard Thompson, himself a fine practitioner of the chiming ballad and the coruscating *aperçu*. The principle difference between the two is Thompson's scintillating brilliance as a guitarist – a plaudit that will certainly never be levelled at the man labelled 'Little Hands Of Concrete'.

As Greil Marcus has observed Costello is 'an original', but it would be closer to the truth to describe him as an original conduit, an absorber and interlocutor of rock and pop history with a peerless ability to mould those strands into a unique, personal language that itself shines with traces of the glittering musical heritage he has so carefully osmosized. A magpie, to put it more brutally.

From the beginning the Costello brand has been a studious amalgam of choice ingredients. His singing voice is a case in point. Nasal and American since before *My Aim Is True*, with more than a hint of fellow Americanophile Graham Parker's throaty rasp, it is a thing of elastic timbre that at one and the same time sounds like several different artists (Bruce Springsteen, Bob Dylan, Randy Newman, Van Morrison) though, simultaneously, always, unmistakably like Elvis Costello.

In some senses Costello is just a hyper-fan. He continues to haunt record shops with the enquiring mind (if larger wallet) of a newly intoxicated seventeen-year-old, a collector's zeal for the arcane nugget and a purist's enthusiasm for lost classics. He would have made a great music critic, ironically, given his suspicion of the trade.

Over the years Costello has been unstinting in his efforts to pass on his knowledge of and enthusiasm for music of every shade. He has often taken up the invitation of radio stations to spin his favourite records over their airwaves – his choices are sometimes surprising and always illuminating. On London's Capital Radio at the height of punk he shattered preconceptions by spinning country and jazz records and waxing lyrical, not for the last time, about Frank Sinatra (he would later pen an informed obituary of the great crooner).

In 1998 he was guest DJ on Dublin's Eclectic Ballroom show, airing tracks by South American protest singer Victor Jara, Dusty Springfield obscurities and even some rum comic asides by Noël Coward. No records by The Knack featured.

At other times Costello has been diligent in his championing of young talent – though he tends to show his age by his preferences, nearly all of whom work in the 'old school', singer-songwriter form. Costello-soundalike Ron Sexsmith is one he, typically, continues to praise, though there have been myriad endorsements over the years, from the understandable – country-punks Rank And File, jazz-inflected indie melancholics Everything But The Girl – to the insouciant, such as Daryl Hall, and plain baffling, ie Wendy James.

But Costello reserves his greatest reverence for artists of the past. Even a spot of guest reviewing for Britain's *Mojo* magazine in 1998 (in whose pages he also eulogized the work of the recently departed David Accles) evinced a musicologist's sense of history. Describing Bob Dylan's return to form opus *Time Out Of Mind* as evidence of a 'living tradition' implicitly echoed his own songwriting métier. He went on to contextualize Dylan as an embodiment of musical evolution itself, describing his hero (and inadvertently himself) as 'every kind of culture mixed up – I mean, what's Robert Zimmerman [Dylan's real name] doing living in Duluth? That's in itself a story. His family had to get there from somewhere. There's folk music explained right there.' Of course, Costello's own Irish musical heritage would make an equally enthralling chapter in the book of musical diasporas.

With these themes in mind it is possible to perceive Costello's truest gift as his ability to blend contemporary concerns with this rich, time-honoured seam of quality songwriting and musicianship. He too can make a tradition live in the present, as Greil Marcus concludes in an article about *King Of America*:

'Within a single tune the time frame may range from the forties to the present, but it never holds still: time folds in on itself. A reference to Madonna's "Material Girl" can sound as dated, as faded, as one to "Smoke Gets In Your Eyes".'

For Elvis Costello music is like air. He wakes up in the morning and it's there, sustaining, invigorating (and occasionally choking) him. He is a true obsessive, with enough God-given talent (and enough past record sales to persuade cash-conscious record companies) to bring his countless new ideas to some sort of real world fruition. Whatever he tries to carry off he generally does so with some sincerity and no little aplomb. That doesn't mean all his creative decisions are good ones – indeed he has become a stranger to critical encomium in recent years, partly because he displays so much energy and puts out so much work of varying style. Critics tend to distrust him, implying dilettante-ism, but it is nearer to the truth to describe him as a 'jack of all trades – master of some'. That he is still trying is his greatest, most under-celebrated virtue.

The final testament to the often brilliant, sometimes perplexing but always intense phenomenon that is Elvis Costello goes to his most recent significant collaborator, Burt Bacharach: 'Elvis Costello is a very unique talent. And a good survivor. He's still standing after all these years. It's been a while.'

INDEX

PICTURE CREDITS

Picture section page 1: Pictorial Press. Page 2 top and bottom: Keith Morris/Redferns. 3 top: Rob Verhorst/Pictorial Press; bottom Keith Morris/Redferns. 4 top and bottom: Keith Morris/Redferns. 5 top: Keith Morris/Redferns; bottom: Patrick Ford/Redferns. 6 top: Jeffrey Mayer/Pictorial Press; bottom: Peter Still/Redferns. 7 top: Rob Verhorst/Pictorial Press; bottom: Pictorial Press. p8: Nicky J. Sims/Redferns.